The all-new
Activity Director's
Bag of Tricks
by
Dennis Goodwin

Revised 2021
Original copyright 2013 by Dennis Goodwin
All rights reserved
dennisgoodwin1947@gmail.com

DEDICATION

To my wife and best friend, Joan, who jump-started me to revise an earlier book, using new ideas and thoughts gleaned during the interim from trial and error (*especially error*) and then helped me every step of the way. As it turned out, I wrote an entirely new book.

And to our cat, Stormy, who sat at my feet during much of the writing - and didn't actually write most of the good parts...*no matter what she said.*

Other Books by the author:

History Makers—volumes 1,2,3,4,5
Out of the West
Brass Bands and Snake Oil Stands
Fate, Flukes & Fame in Country & Bluegrass Legends
Slices of Life

 # Fighting the Burnout Bug & the Documentation Demon

Whether you are fresh off the vine in the activity field or like many of us, a tad withered around the leaves, this little book can help pump fresh nourishment into your roots. A colorful crop of varied programs can do more to lure participants into your activities than all the posters, announcements and begging put together. Variety is definitely the key to success. In many jobs it pays to be a specialist. In the activity area though, since we work with such a wide range of likes and dislikes, if we are going to reach the largest number of residents, we need to "specialize" in being a *generalist.*

Hopefully as you read through the program ideas and tricks of the trade, they will also help to safeguard you from that insidious pest that too often lurks in the field waiting to attack both you and your activity crop. Year-by-year, if you're not protected, he can sneak up, latch onto you and slowly start sucking away much of your initial enthusiasm - the *burnout bug.*

One of the best ways to prevent his nasty bite is to realize that what we often interpret as burnout is usually just a natural response to repetition. It doesn't mean that we're dried up and done for and need to step aside to make room for a more motivated activity director. In fact, we simply need to think back to our childhood for an example of a solution to burnout. What about that favorite candy bar we bought a zillion times in a row? As the weeks rolled by, something happened didn't it? That caramel-nut cluster slowly but surely began to lose its unique flavor. Well, guess what that was? *Burnout!*

So what did we do - swear off candy bars? No, we simply added more variety and reached out to Snickers, Milky Way, and all the rest. Suddenly, something magical transpired with our previously burned out little taste buds. They began happily firing away again. So, just because you see the burnout bug's nasty little mandibles reaching out for you, doesn't mean you need to drop your head in shame and step aside to let a younger fresh-faced activity director pump new blood into the program. Don't worry, his or her little bright-eyed face would also eventually wear the look of thinly disguised monotony.

Obviously adding variety to your programming doesn't include wiping the "three B's" off your calendar (Bingo, Bible study and Birthday parties). But in and amongst these "untouchables" are quite a few programming time-slots that can be rearranged or modified. If your weekly balloon volleyball game has lost its bounce or your twice-a-week Coffee and News Hour doesn't seem quite as newsworthy as it once did, you can always trim down the frequency. Maybe scheduling the balloon bashing once a month would make it seem a little more novel. And once a week might be enough for the coffee-drinking newshounds. After all, they usually read the paper on their own anyway.

And what about that Poetry Corner group that seems to lose its rhythm halfway through the activity, or the Hangman word game that gets hung up after one game? You might consider the concept of creating *Cluster Activities* out of two or three smaller activities. You might want to stop the poetry reading after twenty minutes, move right into a twenty-five-minute word game, then wrap it up with ten minutes of Jokes for the Folks. This will not only add *pizzazz* to the activities themselves but will free up programming time slots.

As with the jokes, a riddle session, maybe called Ridiculous Riddles, seems to work better in ten to fifteen-minute doses. Once again, that's not a problem. Start out with the riddles, move into a twenty-five minute trivia portion and wrap it up with twenty-minutes of Name That Tune (as described on page 134 & 135). There's nothing wrong with programming in back-to-back variable time slots. In fact, using cluster activities will very likely hold the residents' attention more than a full dose of any of the individual activities. As a welcome by-product, it will also help keep you more interested *and interesting*. You can either cluster them as one group - maybe call it Brain-teasers or Thought-ticklers, or list each activity separately. Incidentally, if you program a riddle group, you have to ask them what we would have if everyone in the country drove a pink car. Well - a *pink car nation*, of course. Oh stop your groaning!

As you open time slots by shrinking program frequency and clustering activities together, you can stick in some new activities, which will perk up your schedule and your interest. But what about the "untouchable" activities I mentioned? What do you do when you simply feel you don't have another Bingo game left in you? Well, one thing you might do is to remember the poor mud-caked guy digging the sewer you passed on the way to work this morning. Or how about that Walmart returns girl last night, under attack by that she-devil who probably bought that sweater without the receipt in Kmart six months ago?

Of course there will be times when your work gets tough. That's why they call it *work*. But compared to the sewer guy and the complaint girl, you ain't doin' so bad, huh? Also, remember that even though you may have been through an endless stream of Bingo games, that new lady in room 23 who spent last evening crying about her husband's recent stroke, hasn't. Neither has the retired Air Force jet pilot in room 17 who just learned he might lose his right foot to diabetes.

So, slap on a smile, spin the Bingo cage and *let her rip*! Besides, as most of us have learned, it probably won't be too long before you get caught up in the residents' enthusiasm yourself, especially if you focus on that bright-eyed lady who just came in last Tuesday and hasn't heard any of your Bingo-banter yet. Not only that, but since you've freed up a few time slots, you have that new Human Horse Race to plan for tomorrow. And don't forget, you need to buy dog and cat treats for next Saturday's Best-dressed Pet show. *Hmmmm*, could it be the burnout bug is beginning to back off just a bit?

Now is when the seasoned veterans among us might say, "Okay, maybe opening up some time slots and adding new activities could help fight off the burnout bug - but what about the dreaded documentation demon? It comes swooping down to drop a stifling glob of paper and computer work on me that will smother the life out of my day. I got into this field for the *people-work* not the *paperwork*!" All right, I'll admit it - this one's tougher. But here are some thoughts that might help.

First, don't feel like you are misinterpreting the situation. The truth is, you are absolutely right. But your new pink-cheeked replacement would soon feel the smothering effects of the documentation demon too. Most likely all of us would agree that some of our documentation is logical and useful. We obviously need to assess residents to see what they enjoy and have enjoyed. Also, some kind of attendance record traces their patterns of participation. Quarterly progress notes also seem useful and tend to help us focus on each resident. And a care plan approach sometimes leads to including someone in an activity we might not have previously considered.

So maybe a couple hours out of our eight-hour day need to be dedicated to documentation. That's not too horrible - about the same as a teacher's paperwork, and somehow they have time for quite a bit of people-work during the day. In fact, I compare us to teachers because they have some pretty similar documentation - like class-planning, taking students' attendance and recording their progress.

Despite their required documentation, though, nobody in his right mind would expect them to cancel a class in order to fill out intricate repetitive forms or attend useless meetings. There is an innate understanding that despite the need for documentation, the teacher's actual class work takes time priority. Surely no one would prefer that their favorite teachers had spent more time with paperwork or meetings, rather than helping them wade through those scientific formulas or math problems that had them baffled.

In the activity area, however, especially in nursing homes, that understanding doesn't always exist. Sadly, I can't count the times I have seen talented and caring activity directors wither on the vine because unrealistic documentation and useless meetings had sucked away their emotional nutrition. And nearly every one of them wore the same wistful look as he or she lamented, "This *used to be* fun!" We got into this field to work primarily with people, not computers. If we don't feel the daily reward of a good dose of direct resident contact, we shrivel and die.

In many cases, much of that "smothering glob" of docu-mentation was heaped together by individuals who never actually did the job. The companies that run facilities, the consultants who train the directors and the agencies that survey them should have *one common goal* - to help the director create the best possible department for the residents. Any repetitive or unnecessary documentation requirement thrown in the path of the director impedes that goal. It's not that documenting is particularly difficult or distasteful; it's just that it can too easily crowd out programming time and become the primary focus of your day.

And yes, I am sure that some of the clinically minded folks among us are likely raising their eyebrows right now, saying things like, "If we don't set high documentation standards we will never improve," or "*Document, document, document!*" Well, in response I wave my bony index finger and chant, "Oh no, no, no - *program, program, program!*"

Here, I think, is where we got off track. Although there are sometimes blurred boundaries among them, there are several models of recreation. Two of these are often called the *medical model* and the *community model*. The medical model is more *curative* and concentrates on treating and improving what is *wrong* with the individuals in the program. This model is ideal for treating patients following an accident, prolonged illness or a recent stroke. The community model's focus, on the other hand, is directed more toward enhancing the quality of life and maintaining and improving what is still *right* and functional. One of the best places to observe this model is in your local community senior center.

So, which type of program model is "better" or "more important"? Neither, of course! They are simply different modes of recreation for differing populations. Now, since we're talking about differences, let's look at another vital distinction - the staff-to-participant ratio. In the medical-model setting, the recreation professional often spends considerable time addressing and measuring the improvement of each individual, much like physical, occupational and speech therapists do. Obviously, this requires a much smaller staff-to-patient ratio than the senior center coordinator who often organizes large-group activities and socials. An additional difference in the clinical environment is that when improvement stops, the activity "treatment" also stops. I would love to see what would happen if we discontinued Bingo.

So then, which model should we look toward in considering the nursing home and assisted living recreation programs? Well, I'll give you a hint - when I began as an activity director in 1978, my staff-to-resident ratio was one-to-eighty. When I retired in 2012, it was about one-to-sixty-five. Not a *lot* of difference in 34 years. And of course, this situation is not unusual. In that setting, we have two options. We can develop either a weak medical-model program or a vigorous and varied community-model program.

The choice seems obvious. For one thing, most of the resident's limitations we deal with are primarily the result of natural aging and unfortunately, are not actually *treatable*. We just need to modify the activities and adapt the equipment to meet the declining abilities of the residents. Also, when you think about it, nursing and assisted living centers are *communities* aren't they? They have their own restaurant, laundry, beauty shop and all...so why not their own "senior center?"

But since health care activity directors are working in a primarily clinical environment, the natural tendency of regulators and consultants was often to view the program through the lens of the medical model and emphasize detailed time-consuming clinical documentation. If a company or individual facility wants to provide recreational therapy along with physical, occupational and speech therapies for their short-term rehabilitation patients; more power to them. They simply need to staff it with an appropriate number of certified therapeutic recreation specialists, obtain doctor's orders and document and bill for it accordingly.

I feel, though, that the planning and programming for the long-term residents should be documented and surveyed as a community-based recreation program. That mode should focus more on the quality and variety of the programs offered as well as on the residents' satisfaction and participation - and *much less* on highly detailed clinical documentation.

So you say, it looks like you may have identified the problem, but what's the solution? Well, the best advice I can give a time-pressured activity director is to fight (in a professional manner of course) for every possible minute of potential people-time. If you'll notice, in a nursing home setting, the director of nursing might excuse herself from an extended morning meeting with, "I'm sorry, I have to meet with the west wing nurse." And the dietary supervisor will politely step out of a prolonged care-planning session saying, "Are there any more dietary questions? I'm afraid I need to head to the kitchen to help with lunch." All too often, however, the poor activity director will sit in a run-on meeting, casting nervous glances at his or her watch as the necessary preparation time for the upcoming Luau party dwindles into oblivion.

I'm not suggesting that anyone put his or her job on the line. But through my experience, I've found that by rationally presenting the time-constraints to administrators and to other department heads, you can often whittle away some of the unrealistic time-barriers. Your goal should be to document only essential information in as brief a format as possible and attend only those meetings that are useful or required. Although your supervisor and peers might initially think you are trying to get out of your job, as they see you are attempting to increase the variety and frequency of your activities, they will hopefully realize you are actually struggling to *get into your job.*

And that job, of a modified senior center director, is one of the most important you'll ever find. If you're looking for big bucks, then buddy, you came knockin' on the wrong door. Most of us didn't get into this field for the money, and it's amazing *how well that's worked out for us.* But if you are after a position with big rewards and the ability to make a real difference in people's lives, you found it. All of us have heard family members say, "It takes a *special* type of person to do what you do." Although we are not heaven-sent, there is some truth to that and we should take pride in our unique skills and attributes.

At the same time, it's important to recognize that although our positions may seem unique and special, there are far more similarities than differences when we compare ours with any other job. For one thing, the secret to success in our field, as with all others, is that *there is no secret.* The good old-fashioned qualities that our parents and grandparents struggled to instill in us are still as vital as ever. Enthusiasm, compassion, honesty, courtesy, patience, inventiveness and all the rest still rule. Now, speaking of inventiveness, let's see if we can come up with some cool new stuff to juice up your program.

 **"Staycation" Display**

What it is:

In this large group display and discussion, the residents and staff members get to share souvenirs and memories of past vacations even though they "stay" in one place.

What you will likely need:

You're going to be *hounding* residents and staff members for souvenirs they have collected on vacations or trips to visit relatives. Although some people are more widely traveled than others, most folks have picked up some locally made crafts or various souvenir knick-knacks during family trips, which would add interest to the show. Most of the residents' objects will likely be in the safekeeping of their family members. So you will need to inform the residents several weeks in advance and continue to remind them to ask their kids or grandkids to bring in that metal statue of the Empire State Building or that colorful doll from Mexico, when they come in to visit.

If any residents or staff members were born in another country, this display is a great format for them to exhibit clothing and objects from their previous homeland. Through the years, in fact, the "Staycation" Display concept has led to some great staff and resident interaction. One time a nurse and a nursing assistant, both originally from Africa, demonstrated a lively African board game. At another display, a resident showed a glass bottle of sand he had taken from a desert in the Holy Lands. He told how he had asked the tour guide if he could hop off the bus and get a small sample of sand to take back home with him. After the guide gave his okay, the resident collected it. He was as tickled as if the guide had given him a solid gold bar...even though there were several billion tiny bottles worth of sand in that desert.

You will likely want to make labels to place under each object, saying who loaned it for the show...maybe something like this:

 "Staycation" Display

How it looks:

The participants will be seated in rows facing the display tables, with room in front of each row for you or a volunteer or assistant to walk up and down with the items. The souvenirs are displayed on tables at the end of the room. Plastic tablecloths and a few travel posters on the wall behind the tables can class it up with a minimum of time and energy involved.

What you do:

You will conduct a little interview with each resident and staff member who loaned you a souvenir. I would suggest asking any staff member who is working at the time to try to drop in for a minute or two. You will likely need to keep the schedule loose, jumping to the staff member's display item when he or she can stop by.

Of course the people you are interviewing will run the gambit from quiet shy folks you have to "pry open" with several questions, to those who are convinced that the entire event should focus on their travels. For the quiet ones, you might write down a number of possible questions in advance, like "What sight did you enjoy the most during your trip?" "What made you decide to travel there?" "Did anything unusual happen during your vacation?" "What seemed to be the main difference in people there and here?" and "Were you glad you went there?" And for the ones whose mouths seem to *runneth over*, you can mimic the TV game-show host who cuts off a chatterbox guest with a polite, "Thank you very much - and now let's talk to George."

Incidentally, this concept came about as the time approached for what I had originally conceived as a full-fledged International Day event. As one after another of the staff and family members, who had selected various countries to highlight, seemed to lose enthusiasm, I reluctantly modified the event to this souvenir-display idea. Fortunately, it turned out to be very successful and became a regular semi-annual event. Sometimes it is better to simply lower your expectation-bar a bit rather than trying to push people over a higher one they actually don't want to jump anyway.

"Racemania"

What it is:

This is a modified large-group racing game that several residents throughout the years have told me they enjoyed as much as...(get ready for this)...*Bingo*! In fact, *Racemania* has drawn in several fellows who never set foot in a Bingo game. It is basically the age-old game of horse racing with a few tweaks and twists.

What you will likely need:

You can buy several types of pre-made horse race game sets like this one, which has long been a specialty of Sea Bay Games out of New Jersey.

You can also make your own. In fact, the racing *critters* don't even need to be horses. If you'd prefer, you can hold "Cow Races," "Donkey Races" or "Moose Races." Even if you buy the ready-made horse racing set, you can modify it for various holidays. "Bunny Races," "Leprechaun Races," "Monster Races," "Reindeer Races," "Scarecrow Races," "A Turkey Trot" and others like the ones below, can add a little zest to the holidays.

Once you make one of these holiday race sets, it will be available for years to come. Toy stores, dollar stores and party-supply shops are good hunting grounds for figures to transform into your holiday speedsters. They will need to be large enough to be easily seen.

If you run across figures like the bunnies and monsters on the previous page, you only need to put a number on each one and you're off and running. Incidentally, my monsters were bobble-head figures and the bunnies were originally filled with candy. The reindeer and turkeys were created from Internet pictures printed out (with numbers overlaid) on page-size printable cardstock. It's amazing what pictures you can find using a search engine's "image" function, when you search for terms like "racing reindeer," "running turkey," "racing rabbits" and such.

Once you have located the picture on the Internet, you can simply copy it to a blank word-processing page. I go into this process a bit more in the section dealing with obtaining clip art illustrations for a "memory book" on pages 65 and 66. You will simply need to add a *text box* on top of your racing turkey, reindeer or other critter, and type in a nice large number "1." Print that one out, then change the text box to "2" and so on. After you have printed them all on the printable poster paper, you can simply trim around the pictures and laminate them for longevity.

The most practical bases for your racers seem to be small wooden blocks (available in art and craft stores like Michaels or Hobby Lobby). One block attached to the bottom back of the laminated racer, with 3M or Scotch brand permanent double-sided permanent adhesive, seems to do the trick. You might also use Velcro to make it easy to switch out the various types of racers. You can use the 2" blocks to make them a little less likely to be knocked over, but the 1½" blocks seem to work well enough.

The illustration below shows how a ready-made racing track will likely look. As you can see, there are six lanes with several lines crossing them along the way to the finish line. But we're going to modify that a bit in a minute.

6								6
5								5
4								4
3								3
2								2
1								1

The ready-made set also comes with index-sized cards with a little horse-race design and a large number from one through six. These can be copied using a heavyweight copy paper and cut out so you will have plenty. Similarly, if you have lucked out and conned a friend into making the set, you can make a master for the cards on a computer (maybe using the "table" function at the top of a Microsoft Word page - set for two rows and three columns like the illustration below). After you have printed or copied the page on heavyweight copy paper, cut the cards out. You will be handing these out to the participants before the races start so you will know who receives a payout.

How it looks:

The racetrack can be placed on a long table along the side of the room, with space behind it to walk around and pick up a die thrown under the table. The residents will face the table in a large semicircle around the perimeter of the room. The center of the room should remain open, since this will be the area in which they will take turns throwing the die. A five-inch soft foam rubber die is ideal and can be purchased individually from various Internet game suppliers and school supply companies.

What you do:

I would definitely suggest having at least two of you working this activity. One will begin by handing out the number cards to the participants. You need to have at least one participant selecting each one of the six numbers. Otherwise there will be a horse with no winner. However, as many people can take a particular number as they want to. If you haven't programmed this before, you will likely get a kick out of how many people stick to the same "lucky number" forever.

While one person is handing out the number cards, the other will be naming the horses. Naming them each game (not each race) seems to add fun to the event, although I must admit there have been more than a few disputes over whether a particular horse is going to be named *Hot Shot* or *Zippy* that race. Usually a little *schmoozing* and a coin toss will do the trick.

Once the cards are handed out and the horses are named, it is time for the *games to begin*. A bit of hokey "show biz" always brightens the activity. I would suggest the two activity staff members or a staff & volunteer team throw the first toss. Taking turns with the start of each race, one can throw the die at the other (softly) while he or she holds out a basket to catch it; dangles a cow bell behind a tambourine; slowly swings the tambourine back and forth; takes a (slow and easy) swing at it with a maraca; puts the basket on his head (with a protective hand in front of the face) etc. I know this sounds silly, and of course it is, but it starts each race on a high note.

Beginning with the second toss, the two *racing staff* stay in front of the long table and begin taking the die around the semicircle for each resident, in turn, to toss to the center of the room. And yes, there is quite a bit of bending involved (hence the concept of always having *two staff*). Incidentally, I would strongly advise against scheduling it, as I did several times, for the afternoon following an outing to Atlanta's famous Varsity Restaurant - with its legendary chili burgers and greasy onion rings. *Just sayin'!*

If you are fortunate enough to have three of you (maybe including a visiting grandchild) you can rotate through three positions, with one person standing in back of the track moving the horses and the other two passing the die around the semicircle of residents. You can also have the resident throw the die in a box you are holding, to avoid the bending, but it's not as easy for the other participants to see.

Now, here's one of the tweaks I mentioned earlier. If you are using a track like the one pictured previously, rather than following the exact instructions, I would suggest using *every other line* so you move a horse *two spaces* for each toss. Also, some versions of racing games have you throwing a dice to decide which horse to move and a second one to select the number of spaces it will move, I have had more luck simply making a two-space move for each horse as its number is rolled.

The two-space move keeps the game clipping along at a good pace. The winning horse's number will have to be thrown five times for it to win. In fact, you might keep this modification in mind if you are making the set, and only have three crossing lines between the starting and finish lines - since the move from the starting space to the next space will be the first...and the move from the last space before the finish, to the finish line will be the fifth...like the one below. One method of creating the track is to use a bright-colored ¾ inch Scotch brand electrical tape sold at stores like Home Depot or Lowes, laid out on a sturdy plastic tablecloth. You can also use an Internet company like Vistaprint, to make a reasonably priced vinyl banner that can easily serve as a pretty classy looking track.

6	Start					Finish	6
5	Start					Finish	5
4	Start					Finish	4
3	Start					Finish	3
2	Start					Finish	2
1	Start					Finish	1

As a suggestion, for the race itself, I would have two winners per race, each getting the same amount of money. Quarters work well if your budget can cough them up. Sit down with your calculator and see what you can afford. As an example, if you have about twenty participants, since two of the six horses will win, you'll give about a third of them quarters after each race - about a dollar and a half to two dollars. If you can swing it, you might even give "win, place and show" money for the last race - with quarters for *place* (second place) as well as *show* (third) and maybe even fifty cents for *win*.   Basically, if you use this method with about twenty residents, you be shelling out about $10 a game. If you need to, of course, you can trim it down a bit. If you are *flush with cash* - step it up a little.

From experience, it seems that playing five games is the ideal amount. Now here's another touch of hokey showmanship. When each winning horse crosses the finish line, you and your partner can grab a cowbell, tambourine, maraca or such and make a little noise to celebrate the win. If you have any resident's kids or grandkids visiting the race, they make natural cheerleaders with the noisemakers. In fact, grandchildren also make wonderful die picker-uppers! This game is also an excellent way to involve staff members passing by the room. It's great hearing residents root for the director of nursing or administrator to throw their number...and sometimes giving them a good-natured *boo* if they don't.

At the end of the last game, you can take a "snack wagon" cart around the semicircle for those who want to trade in their quarters for goodies. Small school-lunch sized sacks of chips and Cheetos, Little Debbie snack cakes, packs of crackers and other *healthy* little items are perfect, and they average out to about a quarter each. Don't forget to get several things that diabetic residents can eat. While one staff or volunteer makes the snack rounds, the other can pick up the number cards and sort them for the next game.

Once again, this activity can be a winner, so if you haven't tried it or even if you have and it just didn't seem to take off, give it a shot. As with the activity, Root Beer and Roulette, which I cover later in the book, you will have to explain to reticent residents that they will not be gambling since they are not putting up any money. When you are inviting new residents to join in, you might also let them know that you are aware that senior citizens don't traditionally play with little plastic horses and *whoop* and *holler* as they toss a rubber die. Although I do remember one time when I told a newly admitted lady that the game was "a little silly but a lot of fun." One of our regular race fans was passing by on her way to the game and smiled and told her, "Oh no, it's not silly, *it's just fun!*"

 # Best-dressed Pet Show

What it is:

As the name implies, this is a show full of photo opportunities, as pets (dogs primarily) display their fineries for the residents. And in case you are not a *pooch-apparel* type of person...yes, there *are* a number of folks who have either bought or made sweaters, scarves and such for their pets (or could easily be talked into it).

What you will likely need:

The key ingredient to success in this venture is obviously, recruiting several *best-dressed pets*. A poster and sign-up sheet make a good start for promoting the event, but *only* a start. You will need to *stalk* potential participants in department-head meetings, break rooms, nursing stations, activities, informal family groupings and such. Once the well is primed with a few signatures on your sign-up sheet, it gets a bit easier to con others into bringing in their pets. If you have any visiting pet-therapy groups like Happy Tails or Pet Partners, be sure to get the word out to them.

Some of your most likely pet-lovers will be the children and grandchildren of residents and staff members - and they will need mom or dad to drive them. Since most folks are not available on weekdays, I've found that a Saturday morning or afternoon seems to be a good time to program the event.

Music helps to tie the show together. You can download a number of animal-related songs like "How Much is That Doggie in the Window," "Who Let the Dogs Out?" "Hound Dog," "What's New Pussycat?" "What a Pet! (Pet Show)" and "Gotta Pet Your Pet" to make a CD that can be used every year for the event. Incidentally, annual or possibly semi-annual scheduling is likely the best for this show in order to keep it as a special treat for the residents to anticipate. The songs can be played as people gather, to give a little formality to the show.

You will need presents for the pets. Incidentally, I strongly suggest billing this event as a *show* rather than a *contest*. That is, unless you want to be the cause of a little tear rolling down the cheek of the six-year old blond girl holding Fluffy and his scarf as she watches the poodle in the tuxedo walk away with a blue ribbon. If it's a *show* everybody wins! Dog or cat treats and inexpensive pet toys make perfect gifts.

Be sure to have a camera ready with fresh batteries. Most likely every participant will want an individual picture of his or her pet as well as a group photo. A microphone and amplifier will come in handy when you interview each pet owner. As for the *best dressed* part, most pet shops actually have pet clothing for sale - and I'll guarantee you that several of the pet lovers have already purchased or made sweaters, scarves, or tee-shirts for their little four-legged friends.

How it looks:

So you are likely thinking, "*this* is a natural *outside activity!*" And I'm sure it would be, but I've always held it inside for some reason. Anyway, whichever you choose, the layout would be similar. You will be displaying one pet at a time in front of the audience, so you need a *stage* area up front with a sturdy table to hold the smaller pets so everybody can see them. If you have some relatively portable therapy stairs or could recruit a couple of scouts to bring over their *cross-over bridge*, they both make good "runways" to show off the parading pets. If you have a small group, a semicircle gives everyone a front-row seat. If not, they will be sitting in rows facing the stage area, with walking room in front of each row so the pets can meet & mingle with them at the end of the show. Remember, if you have only two rows, you can *stagger* them so everyone can see well.

You will need an off-stage area for the participants who are waiting their turn in the spotlight. Even if the event is held inside, the waiting area can be outside. You might want to appoint a *Chief Petting Officer* (sorry) to make sure there is always a pet "waiting in the wings" ready to go on stage when you have finished with the previous one.

What you do:

As you introduce each owner and his or her pet, you will ask a few questions like, "How old is Cleo?" "What is her favorite pastime?" "How did the two of you meet?" "Does she have a favorite toy?" and "Does she do any tricks?" After Cleo has strutted her stuff and you or an assistant have snapped a couple pictures and given out the treats and toy - it's time for her to exit and make way for the next *star.* And so it goes, with one pet after the next basking in a chorus of *ooohs* and *aaahs.*

I would ask the owners of the pet just exhibited, not to walk their pets up and down the rows while another one is "on stage." They can either return to the waiting area or quietly watch from the side. After the final pet has been shown, it is time for everybody to gather for a group photograph. And this, of course, is *not exactly t*he easiest part of the activity...but can be the most fun. Actually, the only time I've ever had a pet-to-pet confrontation was when our cat, Punkins, put the fear of God in a nearby Greyhound with a warning hiss.

Remember this is a pet show, not just a *dog* or *cat* show. Also, dressing is optional, so an occasional rabbit, hamster or guinea pig can add spice to the mix. Following the group picture, the pets can be paraded up and down the rows while you and your partner take pictures of any residents who want a photo keepsake with their new furry little friends...like this one.

The "Lives and Times" Display

What it is:

This is a display and discussion on accomplishments and interests of participating residents and staff members. It furnishes a great format to learn more about the people who live and work in your center. You will definitely turn up some fascinating insights about them and sometimes create lasting bonds among individuals with similar interests.

What you will likely need:

You will be looking for items and photographs that will highlight the earlier lives of residents and the off-duty lives of associates. Collections make great displays. A lot of people collected things that would interest the group - like paperweights; miniature frogs, penguins, cats and other critters; various antiques; coins; dolls and such. They are usually glad to display one of more of their *treasures*. In fact, as a word of advice, I would suggest limiting a display of collected items to three or four per person. Otherwise, you might find five cardboard boxes of Barbie dolls on your desk after lunch.

Handwork, artwork, handmade jewelry, various crafts, artistic photographs and other creative projects give us all a view of the unique individuals behind the weathered face and trifocals or the starched white uniform and stethoscope. Through the years, I have seen displays of intricate tatting, watercolor landscapes, woodcarving, pottery, beadwork and other projects that cast a whole new light on their creators.

You will want to make sure that someone is in the room at all times watching over the display, so you will need at least one assistant or volunteer for the event. For additional safekeeping, you can put small items in page projectors and larger handwork projects in dry-cleaning bags as you show them around. In fact, you might be able to sweet talk a dry cleaner into giving you a few bags.

You can rustle up some stuff from staff members (using your best pleading skills) but you will usually need to go through family members for the residents' display items. Very often hand-quilted spreads or embroidered napkins and the like have been given to family members. In most cases, they can be talked into bringing an item in if you let them know it will be protected and they can have it back right after the program.

Remember also, that "a picture is worth a thousand words." A photo of someone with a big string of fish, refinishing furniture, working at a previous job, in a military uniform or the like, also makes a great display piece. This is typically the best way to capture the past for the guys. That being said, I remember an old fellow proudly displaying and discussing knitted hats and scarves that he made for homeless people.

Often residents will have pictures on the wall or in photo albums that display their interests and early family times. Making the rounds the day before the event can often turn up some great display items...with their okay, of course. Pictures of grandchildren graduating from school, children receiving awards and other similar events also fall into the category of *resident interests.*

How it looks:

The display items will be placed on tables along the end wall of the room, with a label beside each person's display. I would suggest making these labels in advance, with a heading and clip-art or generic pictures and a line for their name - maybe like the one on the next page.

 **The Life and Times of**

_____

Be sure to make extra labels for the residents whose family member comes running in just before the activity, saying, "Is it too late to get grandma's embroidery in the show?" Tablecloths and posters can also add a touch of class and professionalism to the display tables. As in the Staycation Display, the "audience" will sit in rows facing the display with enough room in front of each row of chairs or wheelchairs for someone to walk along with the objects.

You might also want to create a page-sized sign to hang on the front of each table - maybe something like this:

What you do:

Select an item from the table to show and discuss. If it belongs to one of the residents, ask him or her to tell a little about it. From experience, I would suggest going to the resident in the row rather than trying to move each presenter to the front of the group. This is where a wireless microphone set is worth its weight in gold (incidentally, they are not *crazy expensive* - about $150 and up, and you might luck out and nab one on eBay for considerably less). The portable amplifiers start at about $100. If you don't have amplification, you will usually need to repeat what the resident said to the rest of the group.

This is a basic wireless microphone setup:

As you conduct a little interview, your partner can walk up and down the rows displaying the craft item, picture, collected object or similar display piece. To keep the activity moving along and to protect the pieces, don't let people hold them. You might tell them that everything will be on display on the tables in the front of the room after the show, so now they will need to "touch with their eyes."

Since residents often don't have a prolonged story to tell, you will likely need to stretch out the time by asking the audience questions related to the display piece. If it's handwork, for example, you might ask how many of them did something similar and whether they preferred embroidery, cross-stitching, knitting, tatting, etc. Since there is a reminiscence aspect to the group, if you need more time while the item makes the rounds, you can take informal polls. You could ask, "How many of you made clothing for your children's dolls?" "Which type of handwork do you think is the most difficult?" or "What type of needlework did your mother do?"

If a participating on-duty staff member is available for a minute, grab him or her and move to their display item. Let them know before the show starts that you'd like to have them drop in for a couple minutes when they can. From experience, even the shy nursing assistant who says she doesn't have anything to say and mumbles, "I just collect dolls," will usually blossom out when you or the residents inquire further. Question like, "When did you start your collection?" "What was the first doll you ever collected?" and "What made you start your collection?" will usually break through the initial reticence and tap into her enthusiasm for the hobby. This display *takes a little doin'* but you will learn a lot of new and fascinating things about the people you see every day.

A Modified
"Price is Right" Game

What it is:

This is a modification of the television game, that works well with a large group of residents. I tinkered and tweaked it through the years until it became one of the most popular activities in the program. In fact, whenever I worked on a Saturday, I traditionally programmed it for the morning activity, for no particular reason other than I'm a bit of a creature of habit. After doing this for a few months, I overheard one resident asking another what they would be doing tomorrow (a Saturday). The answer, a resounding, "Why, the Price is Right, of course!" let me know I'd better keep it as a regular gig.

What you will likely need:

You will need either a dry-erase board or a flip chart on an easel to keep track of the guesses. Rather than using actual objects, you'll be making *game sheets,* using pictures from advertisements in Sunday newspapers and mail-out flyers from K-Mart, Walmart, Sears, Macys, Home Depot and such. You can either cut them out and stick them on page-sized poster board sheets or create them on a computer. Since you will need quite a few, however, the computer-made version can run through a lot of ink,

If you include some of the accompanying write-up with the brand name and a brief description, you will be able to read it aloud so the participants will know exactly what they are guessing on. You will not be handing the sheet to the residents, since you have the price on the reverse side - but merely holding it in front of them. On the backside of the sheet, write the price in small numbers along with a price range - like: *$5 to $25*. Incidentally, I actually had one resident who would try to sneak a peek at the back of the sheet, so I would suggest writing a couple of fake numbers in front of the price. Here's a sample game sheet, and yes, it's a *Johnie* – a little humor spices up any activity. In case you are wondering, the "actual retail value" is $437.00 – a rather pricey throne!

THE PRICE IS RIGHT

Caroma Water Saving Toilet from Sears
(This one is a "Luxury" model.)
range: from $300 - $500

Creating these game sheets provides a good project for volunteers, family members, kids, *strangers passing by on the sidewalk* or basically anybody you can con into it...since it *is* time-consuming. If you have access to a digital slide projector, you can create sheets on computer files and project them on a screen. You will also want to number six index cards ("1" on one, "2" on another, etc.) You'll hand these cards to the participants to keep track of who's playing that particular game.

How it looks:

The illustration on the next page shows the layout for the board. On the dry-erase board or flip chart, mark off six columns and five rows like the illustration on the next page and write a number (1 through 6) above each column. Use the whole board or page for this so it is easy to see. You will be filling in the spaces with the participants' guesses. I suggest playing ten games, so you'll need to erase and re-mark the dry-erase board or use a second easel-pad sheet halfway through the game.

1	2	3	4	5	6
2.99	3.50	4.00	1.75	3.75	4.10
25.00	20.00	15.00	16.95	12.75	13.00
7.99	12..50	15.00	13.95	8.50	11.75
13.59	20.00	17.95			

The participants can be arranged in a large semicircle, facing the easel. Twenty-four or less works best, simply because you will only be working with only six at a time and it would be a considerable wait for their turn if there were more. It's interesting, though, how involved many of the residents get who are not actively guessing - rooting the players on (and "moving them along" if they are taking too much time to guess). The game cards, calculator, quarters or prizes and markers will be on a table beside the easel.

What you do:
Hand out the six numbered index cards, in order, to the first six participants in the semicircle - beginning either way you'd like. You can try differing amounts of contestants, but from my experience, six seems to work

best - fewer seem to slow the game and more gets confusing. In fact, if you have a very large resident population, you might even consider capping the group at eighteen or twenty-four and programming more than one group at various times or days - using different residents. When the first six have played, pass the six cards on, in order, around the circle. Don't worry about having a group divisible by six...just keep passing cards around after each game. The players will simply have different numbers in the next game, which is fine.

Let everyone know that there are a couple differences in this version and the television game. First, rather than awarding the "closest guess without going over," you will be giving a prize to the closest guess from *either over or under* the price. Otherwise, there would likely be games in which everyone overshoots the actual price and nobody would win.

You might also let them know that the other distinction is that on TV the contestants win new cars, trips to Europe and large-screen televisions. But in this game "you win fifty-cents and you're happy with it." The amount of prize money or small gifts, of course, is up to you and your budget. Since I have found that ten games seems to fit the time-period well, I would usually give fifty-cents for each game and seventy-five cents if someone got it right on the penny. For the last games, if you are "flush with cash," you might kick it up to 75-cents and a dollar for a right-on-the-money guess.

I say last *games* because you will want everyone to have a chance at the larger amount. Remember you are working in groups of six, so each group of six needs to have their shot at the "big money round." Otherwise you will have some legitimately disgruntled folks. Basically, you can figure on kicking out eight or nine bucks during the activity, since you will likely also have a couple ties that will require paying double money (*no*, you don't want to be a *Cheapo*, and split it in half).

Now, select one of the game sheets and read the information about the item, including the brand name. Then briefly show the page to the six residents holding the index cards. Going back to the number "1" card-holder, show him or her the front of the sheet and ask for a price guess between the range written on the back, like "from five dollars to twenty-five dollars." Giving them the range not only focuses the players on a logical amount but also helps alleviate possible embarrassing guesses miles away from the actual price.

If a participant's guess is way off base, like fifty-dollars for a bag of potato chips, you can often smooth over potential embarrassment with humor, like saying, "Let me run to the store and buy some. I'll sell you *two bags* for fifty dollars." Nonverbal residents can participate by nodding when you list possible prices in increments. For example, you might split up the $5 to $25 item with "Five dollars, seven-fifty, ten dollars, twelve-fifty and so on." If they nod agreement, you haven't put words in their mouth, just helped them guess.

As each resident guesses in turn, you or a volunteer will write that amount in the appropriate block...moving horizontally along the row. When all six bids have been made and recorded, you can circle the winning amount and announce it with a little fanfare, like "The actual retail value of the 10-ounce bag of Lays potato chips is $3.39. The closest guess is *number four!*" Incidentally, unless you are a math wizard, you will likely want to carry a calculator in order to figure the closest guess from above or below the price. As you put away the game sheets you used, I would suggest paper-clipping them together so you won't grab any of them in the near future...since some folks will begin to memorize them.

 # Music & Memories

What it is:

This group combines a reminiscing discussion group, an antique & collectable display and a musical presentation. It works well in a large-group setting as well as in a small group version for memory-impaired individuals.

What you will likely need:

For the "memory" aspect of the activity, there is nothing much better for triggering reflection than actual objects to view and handle. There are several ways to get your hands on some inexpensive (and sturdy) memory-triggering items. Garage sales and flea markets often have some useful goodies like kitchen gadgets, old tools, toys and such. Even the classy antique shops often carry vintage postcards and advertisements, fountain pens, medicine and soda bottles, inkwells and similar things for a reasonable cost. Items like P & G or Fels-Naptha laundry bar soap, Prince Albert pipe tobacco tins and Black Draught laxative boxes are sure to trigger memories. Remember, you don't need display-quality items. A few scratches and dents don't hurt at all. You will need about a dozen display objects for a show.

As to the musical aspect of Music & Memories, you have a couple of options. The best is also, unfortunately, the most expensive - playing old records on a replica phonograph. There are several replica phonographs available that play 78, 33 1/3 and 45 RPM records. Companies like Jensen and Crosley make a number of sharp-looking replica vintage phonographs like the ones on the next page, for about $ 50 to $150.

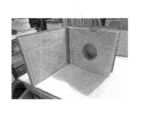

The garage sales, flea markets and antique shops will often have old records. Through the years, I have collected quite a few 78-RPM records for about a dollar each. They will occasionally have the record storage albums to keep them in, like the one in the above-left picture. These, in case you're not old enough to remember them, were usually made of pasteboard and hold a dozen or so records in paper sleeves. They furnish a great way to store the records so they won't get scratched up.

The other musical option, as you might have guessed, is simply to use a CD player. There are quite a few CD's available with collections of songs from the 40's, 50's & 60's that would work well. You might also download and burn specific songs. I would suggest using a variety of musical styles rather than only big band, crooners, jazz or other genres.

How it looks:

If you have a small enough group, a semicircle layout facing a table with the antiques, gives everyone a front-row seat. If not, you can seat the participants in rows with room in front of each row for you to walk up and down with the objects, as in the Staycation Display. The antiques and the replica phonograph can be placed on a table and the records (in a storage album if possible) on another. If you are in a health care setting, an over-bed table works well since you can adjust it to your height. As with most groups, the use of a microphone and an amplifier helps you reach the hearing impaired...and keeps you from straining your voice to the point you don't sound natural. (In case you haven't yet noticed, I *love* P. A. systems).

What you do:

Begin by selecting an antique from the table and briefly explaining its use. You might need to hit the Internet for a little information if you're not familiar with it. If you know basically what the object is, you can use the "images" setting on a search engine like *Google* to find it and can then connect to the image's website for a little more information.

You might begin, for example, with an old box of laundry starch and a bottle of bluing. After you have introduced them and talked a little about them, tell the participants that you will be taking the object around for a closer look while you put on a vintage record. Be sure to tell them the name of the song and the singer or group that recorded it. The music will give residents something to enjoy while you are coming around to them with the antique. As you make your rounds, you can ask the participants if they remember boiling starch or using bluing in their laundry. Obviously you can't spend a prolonged period with each resident, so if someone has an interest in a particular item, they can inspect it further after the show.

Another method, which moves the group at a little faster pace, is to enlist a volunteer to carry the antique around while you talk about it and ask questions of the participants. You will likely elicit some great stories. You can also take "polls" about their shared experiences. For example, if the volunteer is walking around with an old wooden butter mold, you could ask, "How many of you helped your mother make butter?" You might also ask what they thought of oleomargarine, as margarine was originally called, and if they remember mixing a capsule of yellow die with it to turn it from a milky white to a yellow color. Don't worry, even if you are not aware of these things, the residents will soon inform you.

Incidentally, in this case though, even the residents might not know why the oleomargarine companies didn't simply color their product in the factory. The reason being, that the dairy lobby pressured congress into passing a law that their new competitor had to sell their product in the state it was originally produced. They figured the consumer would pass on the sickly white stick and continue to buy real butter. In a clever counter move, the margarine folks included a capsule of dye for the buyer to turn it into a more appealing yellow mixture.

If you are going to use the format of having a volunteer carry the items around while you prompt discussion, you will likely want to play the old records only as the participants gather for the group and then again as they leave. In this way, the music won't overshadow the reminiscing session. I have also had some great luck including middle-school kids in the group. Scout troops are naturals as well, and could work toward a history or heritage-related *Interest* badge. They usually have some insightful questions about earlier times, and the residents' memories become a "living history" lesson for them.

As you continue to gather more display objects, as well as vintage records, you will be able to program the event more often. You could also try to talk others into coming in to show their favorite items. Sometimes you'll luck out and find a staff member who collects interesting antiques or collectibles. Individuals who sell antiques in local consignment shops might consider coming in for a volunteer visit with some of their favorite things. As most of us have found, potential volunteers are sometimes out there just waiting to be asked.

Fabulous Follies

What it is:

This is a form of talent show, and organizing a talent show might seem like a piece of cake...until you try to plan one. In reality, unless you are fortunate enough to have a facility brim full of outgoing talented folks, that cake can be a little tough to slice. Simply posting a flyer and a sign-up sheet is a good start but will usually not result in more than a couple of signatures. Most people would love to see your follies, but not necessarily *love* to be in them.

What you will likely need:

You will need to wear your best salesperson face and take your sign-up list around. In the department-head meeting, explain that if some of them will join in, it will help to prime the pump for others. Then, during the next few weeks, you can rustle up potential talent in the break-room, at nursing stations, during activities and as you talk with family members. Asking individuals about specific performances they might give will shake more fruit out of the tree than a generic talent-recruiting poster alone, but creating a poster & sign-up sheet are the first steps...

The Fabulous Follies

Thursday, March 8th
@ 3:00 p.m.

Sign up <u>now</u> →

Follies Sign-up Sheet		
Name	Act	Time

As you use the necessary attributes of all good activity directors, *begging and pleading*, suggest that people team up as an "act." The nursing assistant who wouldn't dream of doing a solo spot might be coaxed into becoming part of the South Wing's *Southern Belles* dance group...step-dancing to a lively Michael Jackson song. If you can get the North Wing staff to team up, maybe as the *North Stars* and compete with them - all the better. Similarly, a piano-playing family member might consider providing accompaniment to the gospel-singing nurse on the evening shift, even if he or she wouldn't want to perform solo. As you whine and beg, be sure to emphasize the concept that the show is *just for fun* and "there won't be anybody there but *us*."

As with the Best-dressed Pet show, I would suggest calling the event a *talent show* rather than a *talent contest*. Pitting a group of dancing nursing assistants against a resident's flute-playing granddaughter is not only an apples-and-oranges comparison; it's a recipe for emotional disaster. If everyone gets a small keepsake present for performing, *everybody wins*.

How it looks:

Basically, one end of the room will become the "stage" area, with the *audience* in rows, facing toward the entertainers - unless you are fortunate to have an actual stage. If you'd like to add a touch of the old-time variety show, you could use an easel and put up a sign for each act. You can use poster boards printed with a large magic marker (with a different act on each side to save a little money). You could also use a flip chart with the acts written on separate pages. You might even want to add a little of the flavor of the old-time Medicine Shows by having someone peddle *Snake Oil* and a variety of other magical elixirs in between the performances.

What you do:

The "master of ceremonies" (you, most likely) will introduce each act and present a small keepsake present when they finish. Of course a Fabulous Follies talent show is going to be full of photo opportunities so make sure your camera is ready and you have extra batteries. Most of the participants would love to have a picture of their act.

If you have a resident chorus, even if it's not highly formalized, it can become one of the acts. From experience, it's more practical to have them sing from their seats in the audience rather than trying to shift around and get them all up front. Also, if you have a microphone and amplifier, you will need it. That morning-nurse's daughter who is going to read her prize-winning essay, is likely going to get nervous and drop her voice too low for the residents to hear.

Speaking of children, scheduling the Follies from about 3:00 until 4:00 p.m. seems to work well. Parents or grand-parents will have time to pick up their little performers at school and drive them directly to the show. Also, this time period will let a 7-3 staff member perform right after change-of-shift. In fact, you will likely want to keep the schedule flexible, much like the Life and Times display - introducing performers in the order they are able to break free from work or drop in from school.

Remember this if you plan to make a little program for the show, and don't list exact performance times. In fact, the secret to maintaining your sanity with the Follies, as with many other events, is to gripe and grumble *only in your mind* about any mishaps or disappointments. Then, when it's over, you can bask in the glory and act as if it went *exactly* the way you wanted it to.

 **Root Beer & Roulette**

What it is:

This one started out as a small men's group and evolved into a pretty popular open-attendance activity that can be a regular monthly or bi-monthly event. It involves two of the biggest draws of human kind – eating and gambling. Of course, it is not actually gambling since nobody puts up any money. In fact, since Roulette *is* a hard-core gambling game, I would suggest giving only snacks or small prizes rather than quarters, so nobody feels like they've stepped into the "devil's den."

What you will likely need:

In the original men's club activity, I simply used a 16-inch Roulette wheel and felt game layout on a long table. These are available in stores or on the Internet. One company that makes a relatively reasonable version is called Trademark Poker. The wheel itself is about $25 and the green felt cloth with the Roulette layout, runs about $15. The felt, incidentally, should be treated with Scotchgard protective spray (I used an entire can) to make it relatively *root beer and Coke resistant.*

As the "root beer" part of the title implies, sodas and snacks are a vital part of the activity...and are often the main attraction. In addition to root beer, of course, you can serve Cokes and anything else you'd like. Although I resisted for years, you might want to serve only sugar-free drinks in your activities. If an individual is adamant about having a real-sugar drink, you can have some in the fridge ready to bring in. For years I put various markers by residents with diabetes - and for years, volunteers traditionally overlooked them as they poured regular Cokes in the diabetic residents' cups. After countless times of hearing, "Oops, I've already poured her drink; should I take it away?" while a wild-eyed resident clutches her cup for dear life, I've reluctantly given up my "residents' sugar-rights" campaign. The snack part of the activity consists of goodies like potato chips, Cheetos, Funyuns, popcorn and other munchies. A little cart for the drinks will come in handy. As with any snack group, you will need plastic cups, paper plates, napkins and trash bags.

Incidentally, the reason I expanded the men's group to an open-attendance activity was that even though my assistant provided an alternate activity for the ladies, they *crashed* the men's group. The snacks, of course, lured them in. After starting the group with a couple men jokingly assigned as "girl-guards," we soon broke down the barriers and welcomed in the fairer sex.

With the expanded group, it became obvious that we would need a larger roulette wheel. After seeing a large wheel in action at a local church's Men's Club Casino Night fundraiser, we were able to persuade one of the club members to make us one for the cost of the supplies and a small gift. As you can tell from the picture on the next page, it is much easier to see, since it faces the room rather than lies horizontally. The large wheel is on ball bearings to give it free movement. The thirty-six pegs on the wheel correspond to the numbers of the Roulette felt on a nearby table.

After we painted the wheel, I downloaded a picture of a Roulette wheel from a website found with Google's *images* function, enlarged it at a local copy shop and attached it to the wheel with double-stick adhesive. The numbers are simply stick-on numbers and can be purchased at an office supply shop. The face of the wheel can then be painted with an acrylic clear protective coating. Incidentally, the little flap at the bottom that flutters against the pegs of the wheel is simply a piece of plastic cut from a milk or juice carton. It has the perfect flexibility and can be replaced when needed.

There are several plans for upright game wheels available on the Internet. Some of them use the simple concept of attaching a ball-bearing Lazy Susan turntable to the back of the game wheel: wikihow.com/Make-a-Prize-Wheel - crafts.creativebug.com & u-createcrafts.com all have plans. Building the wheel would make a good project for a high-school shop student. As with our men's-club woodworker, you would pay for the supplies and provide a little gift or a small "salary."

There are also a couple of pre-made upright wheels available. They are 24-inch tabletop versions from the companies, Kegworks or Brybelly, and retail for a little under $200. Again, you might find a used one on eBay. There are full-sized upright wheels available as well if you don't mind mortgaging your home to buy them. You will also need to buy some cool-looking poker chips - more about those later.

How it looks:

In a small-group setting, you will simply put the wheel and felt in the middle of a long table and seat the participants around it. In the larger version, the wheel will be at the end of the room, while the residents sit at tables facing the wheel if possible. Since you will be announcing the numbers, a player can face away from the wheel and still participate. You will likely also have several participants around the long table with the Roulette felt layout.

What you do:

As for the Roulette part, you will simply modify the actual game. Anyone who has played it knows it is a relative complicated gambling game. The individuals betting can play blocks of two, four, six numbers and more or wager on red or black; even or odd and other options. This is the basic felt layout:

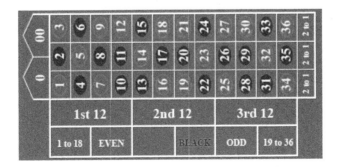

For this activity, I would suggest using only the *block of six* option. For example, in the illustration below, the person betting would win if the number on the wheel is anything from "4" to "9." Let's say it is "8." You'll put a marker on that number.

6	9
5	●
4	7

In the example below, he or she would win if it is anything from "13" to "18." Let's say it is "14." Oh, don't give me that "I can't understand this stupid game, so I'll just flip to the next idea" attitude. It's really not *that* complicated, just difficult to describe. Stick with me. It'll actually make a pretty cool addition to your schedule.

15	18
●	17
13	16

Now, after you've handed out the snacks, with the help of an assistant or volunteer, you will assign number-blocks to the participants. Ask each person in the room, in turn, if they want to bet "high," "low" or "in the middle." This will speed the game along much faster than asking for specific blocks of numbers. If the person says, "high," You might ask them if it would be okay if you gave them "28 through 33." In most cases they'll say "fine" and you will place a plain chip with their name on it, at the bottom of that block of six...like the illustration on the next page. As you can see, the chip is at the bottom of the block, in the middle.

30	33
29	32
28	31

Moving to the next person in the room, repeat the process. If they say they want to place their bet on a "low" number, you might ask them if they want "1" through "6" or possibly "4" through "9." I know this is starting to sound confusing, but what you are trying to do is to make sure that all the six-number blocks are taken. For example, if someone has already taken the "1" through "6" block, you would say, "How about 4 through 9?" If they agree, place a chip with their name on it at the bottom middle of that six-number block. The reason for this is that if all the six-number blocks are not taken, you might have a spin where nobody wins anything. Now, don't get confused about the term *chips*. These are not the poker chips you will use later to pay off the winners. The only reason I use a plain chip with the resident's name on it, is because they are heavier than small pieces of paper and stay in place.

So, still with me? Now, even though you are trying to fill all the six-number blocks, more than one person can take the same block. A lot of times, friends will both want to take the same numbers. That's fine. You will simply put both chips under the block like this. In fact, it's okay to have three or four folks selecting the same six-number block.

30	33
29	32
28	31

The chips with their name on them can be prepared ahead of the game in addition to some blank chips and a fine-point magic marker to make chips for folks you didn't predict would drop in. The red chips most of us have used for Bingo, work fine. Again, remember these are not the poker chips you will be giving out later. They are simply there to identify which residents bet on that six-number block. You will not move these chips during the entire game, unless somebody wants to change their bet (between spins of course).

So hopefully you are starting to get a picture of the action. If not, don't worry - just do a few practice runs and I think it will start to make sense. There will be no other chips on the felt. You will simply use one "marker" of some kind, to place on the number that matches the one the wheel selected. This marker will help you in deciding the winners. Now, here's where it again gets a little tricky to picture, but this will also become clearer with a few practice runs. There will be an overlapping row between the two blocks of numbers.

In the illustration below, for example - if the number selected by the wheel is "14," both the blocks "10" through "15" and "13 through "18" will win, since the number "14" falls in both groups. In other words, the row with the winning number as well as the rows on each side wins. Therefore, you are actually looking at a "block of nine" with the name-chips below the three rows in that block all winning. That isn't the case, of course, if the number is 1 through 3 or 33 through 36, since they are at the ends of the felt layout.

9	12	15	18	21
8	11		17	20
7	10	13	16	19

In order to pump in a little more of the casino flavor, the winners will be paid in poker chips. These chips, unlike the name-marker plain chips, are going to look as much like actual casino poker chips as possible. With the popularity of games like Texas Hold'em and various poker games, several stores like Walmart, Kmart, Target and others carry some pretty classy looking poker chips. These chips will mimic the actual gambling chips, with various colored designs printed on them. You can give out whatever number of chips-per-win that you want, depending on how many chips you're able to buy. I would suggest valuing all of them the same, even if they have different amounts printed on them. It gets truly com- plicated if you don't. In fact, they can all be *$1,000 chips* to add a little of the real casino flavor to the event.

At the start of the game, let everyone know that the "top winners" will receive prizes. I would suggest maybe the top two-fifths. As an example, if you have twenty-five players, the Top Ten will win. You are going to select the winners at the end of the game by the writing down the amount of chips each person won. If you are going to give out more than one chip to each winner, suggest that they keep their winnings in the stacks you hand to them for each winning spin. If you have enough chips to do this, it makes it look more casino-like for them to get a small stack of three or four rather than one chip when they win.

It usually requires at least the first fifteen minutes to get everyone's six-number-block choices marked off and to hand out the snacks. Then the game begins. One person will spin the wheel and one sits at the table with the Roulette felt. When the number is called out after the wheel stops, the person at the table will call out the names of everyone who selected a six-number block that includes the number. A microphone and amplifier will come in handy for this as with most groups. Remember, the winners include not only those names under the row with the selected number, but the row on either side. The "table-worker" can hand out a chip or chips to the winners around the long table, while the "wheel-worker" (and a volunteer if possible) will hand out chips to those at other tables. Of course the *casino workers* can change places whenever they want to.

Once everyone is paid, the wheel is spun again and the process starts over. After about twenty minutes, it's a good idea to take an *intermission* and freshen up the drink cups and snack plates. Then, it's time to begin the final stage of the game. I would suggest playing another ten spins with the last one being a "double-money" spin in which the winners collect twice the usual amount. At the end of the game, the chips or stacks of chips are counted and the Top Ten (or whatever amount you decided on before the game) will be able to select prizes. These don't need to be extravagant - usually individually wrapped Honey Buns, Little Debbie snack cakes, packs of crackers and similar goodies will suffice.

A little Los Vegas "casino chatter" adds to the atmosphere. Comments like, "The bet's are down, let's spin the wheel!" "And...the *winning number* is...*nineteen!*" "We have a *winner!*" and "*One thousand dollars* goes to everybody in the winning number-block!" add a touch of *razzle dazzle* to the activity. Again, I know this is a little tricky to soak up, but I think it's worth the effort. If it seems too confusing, you might ask a *gambler* to help you sort it out.

A "Fun" Fundraiser

What it is:

A *Raffle Auction* lets the residents take an active role in raising funds. It is along the lines of a silent auction but is a lot more fun. Basically it involves holding a series of little raffles and usually gets folks pretty excited when you call out the winners. The event is also known as a Penny Social, Chinese Auction, Tricky Tray or Pick-a-Prize. I originally scheduled it as a one-time thing, but after a few months, people began to ask, "When's the next auction? I've got some stuff to donate." It seems to work well as a semiannual event, held in April or May so the "spring cleaners" can donate the *treasures* they've uncovered - and again in late November to catch the Christmas stocking-stuffer buyers.

What you will likely need:

You will be collecting donated "white elephants" for the event, so post a few flyers and begin spreading the word and explaining the concept at least a month ahead. You can let staff, volunteers, residents and family members know that no item is too small for the auction because an inexpensive donation will be grouped with others. Just as with recruiting talent for the follies or items for the *Staycation* and *Lives and Times* displays, face-to-face contact always trumps posters and announcements.

During the event, you will be placing a cup by each object or grouping of small objects so participants can take a chance by dropping one or more tickets into a cup. The 16-ounce plastic drinking cups at your local grocery store work perfectly for this. You will also need to buy a roll of double-tickets like those used for door prizes. In addition, you'll need a few ballpoint pens, a little cash box, several

51

tables to display the items, and a long table for the resident ticket-sellers. You will also need to buy some removable stick-on "dot" labels from an office supply store. A fairly large bowl will work for mixing the tickets so someone can draw a winner. We traditionally used a plastic Halloween pumpkin basket, since it was the ideal size with a fairly small opening in the top so the tickets don't fly out when mixed. Make sure a small wastebasket is handy to throw the tickets away after each drawing.

Since the associates will comprise a good part of your participants, I would suggest two things. First, hold the event on a payday and secondly, make some I.O.U.s. I know some associates use direct deposit, but in many facilities, there is still a pretty good crowd on payday afternoon. Business-card sized I.O.U.s can be made on a sheet and copied and cut out. They will simply need lines to write the amount and both their printed name and a signature (since many folks have hard-to-read signatures) as well as the date the I.O.U. needs to be paid.

Of course, it's up to you if you want to use I.O.U.s but from experience, you will get a lot more participation. I've never been "stiffed" with nonpayment, but have had to give several *gentle reminders*. For those people I knew would take it in good humor, I occasionally posted a *Raffle Auction Arrest Warrant* like the one on the next page. This was created and saved on a computer file - complete with a clip-art picture of a convict behind bars and the wording: "Raffle Auction Arrest Warrant. Be on the lookout for (their name) and armed and dangerous Raffle Auction payment evader."

Usually within minutes of adding their name to the sheet, printing it out and posting it in their work area, I would receive the crumpled arrest warrant and full payment on my desk, as their coworkers laughed and exclaimed "Oh no he *didn't!*"

Raffle Auction
Arrest Warrant

Be on the lookout for
John Doe
an armed and
dangerous
Raffle Auction
payment evader

How it looks:

The donated items will be displayed on tables throughout the room with space for people to maneuver in amongst them. You will need one long table along the side of the room with enough space for two or three residents to sit behind the table. This will become the ticket-selling station.

What you do:

Even if you are not familiar with this type of fundraiser, you might have been mentally piecing together the concept as I discussed the things you'll need. Basically, it consists of a series of mini-raffles. If a donated item seems fairly valuable, it will be raffled by itself. In many cases, however, several small objects can be grouped together. You can partition the items by running removable "painter's" tape (the blue stuff) along the table between them.

You will need most of the morning to set up, so hopefully you will have an assistant or volunteer to do a morning activity in another section of the building. If the room where you'll hold the event has a door, I'd advise closing it and posting a *kind but firm* do not disturb sign. If not, you will likely need to place a portable curtain or other barrier at the entrance or entrances. Otherwise, your concentration will continually be interrupted with pre-event snoopers asking how it will work.

Now, here's the set-up. Once you have placed all the donated items on the tables so you can see what you have, arrange them so there is at least one eye-catching goodie at each table. When you group the smaller things, you will logically want to put related items together - like earrings with a necklace, salt and pepper shakers with a napkin holder and so on.

Once everything is laid out, you will place one of the 16-ounce plastic cups within each partitioned area. Before you begin setting up, number each of the plastic cups with a marker, starting with "1." You will likely need 50 or 60. Now, here's where the removable dot labels come in. You will have pre-numbered the labels as well. Once you set a numbered cup in the area sectioned off by the blue tape, place a corresponding numbered label on the item or one of the items. Don't worry about keeping the cups in numerical order; it doesn't make any difference at all. If the cup is number 34, just stick the label numbered 34 on the item. The only reason to use the dot stickers is to keep the correct cup by the item or items. Now and then someone might pick up the cup to put in a ticket and set it back in the wrong area - which can create havoc since you wouldn't know who was bidding on which item.

Like the Roulette instructions, I know this might seem a little confusing but it really isn't once you sort it out. I would suggest allowing about forty-five minutes for people to buy tickets and place them in their selected cups. If you begin selling tickets at 2:15 p.m. and start the raffles at 3:00, associates working a 7 to 3 shift can usually stay for a couple minutes while you raffle off an item they bid on.

Instruct the ticket-buyers to separate their tickets and keep the one reading, "keep this side." They may put as many tickets in one cup as they want, since this will increase their odds. It is interesting to see personality differences as people put their tickets in the cups. Some will buy five-dollars worth, separate them and place them all in the cup by one item they particularly want. Others will put one here, one there, two here and so on to spread out their chances on a variety of items.

The cost of the tickets is up to you. You will likely include more people if they are a quarter each or five for a dollar; but you will probably make more money if they are fifty-cents each or three for a dollar. Even though the double tickets have the same number on each ticket, so the winner is easily identified, most folks like to write their name or initials on the ticket they deposit. This way, even if they are working out on the floor, you can get word to them that they have won. Then when they're free for a minute, they can come flying in to claim their treasure, and flaunt it in front of coworkers who competed for it.

It will make life a lot easier during the event if you and the resident ticket-sellers separate the tickets into strips in advance - either five or three, depending on whether you're selling them five or three for a dollar. You might also want to put a few dollar bills and quarters in the cash box for change (and subtract the amount from the profit later).

When you think you are ready, make a last-minute check to see that all the items are laid out either individually or in clusters within the strips of blue tape - along with a corresponding numbered cup. Then check the ticket table to make sure it is stocked with about fifty pre-separated ticket strips (three or five, depending upon the price), a cash box, a few quarters and dollars for change, as well as a number of I.O.U.s and pens to fill them out and to write names on the tickets.

Now, when it's time to start - let's say at 2:15 p.m., the ticket-sellers begin. And that is also when the *questions* begin. You could have six-foot neon flashing signs explaining the concept but, trust me, there will be some folks (department heads among them) standing there with tickets in their hand and perfectly blank expressions on their faces, asking "so what do I do now?" Rather than rolling your eyes in exasperation, simply slap on your eternal-patience smile. Then you can let them know they will need to tear the strip of tickets in half, keep the ones that read "keep this side," separate the remaining tickets and place one or more in the cups by items they want to take a chance on. Even if they have already deposited some of the "keep this side" tickets it's not a problem as long as they don't put both tickets in. If you see a cup with a string of several attached tickets (which you will) simply separate each one and put them back into the cup.

Throughout the ticket selling, you will need to repeatedly explain the concept and roam around making sure cups aren't moved. About fifteen minutes before raffle time, search for empty cups. If you find any, take the cup away and move the item or items into another taped-off section. Be sure to remove the numbered dot sticker so it doesn't get too confusing. This way, you will make sure each donated article can be raffled. It would be embarrassing if nobody bid on something an individual donated.

People can still buy tickets and bid on items even after you start raffling things off, but after forty-five minutes, you will ask those in the room what they would like you to raffle first. Pour all the tickets from the cup into the bowl (or plastic pumpkin basket). After you have stirred the tickets well, ask a resident, family member or staff member in the room to draw the winning ticket. Make sure they didn't put any tickets in the cup for that item. If they select more than one ticket, have them close their eyes and choose a winner from the two or three they originally picked out.

If the ticket has a name or initials written on it, read it off and give the item to the winner if they are in the room. If there is no name, call out the ticket number. If nobody claims the ticket, (which will often be the case, since most associates will be working) attach it to the item with a strip of the blue tape from the table and move on to the next raffle. Be sure to clear all the previous tickets from the bowl each time.

And so the auction goes...with one raffle right on the heels of another, until everything has been raffled off. Any *treasures* that have not been claimed can be stored in the activity room for a while. If they are not claimed within a week, it's likely that nobody really wanted them and they can be given away to whoever might want them.

One good use for the profit made from the Raffle Auction is to schedule professional entertainers you might not usually be able to afford. Of course you could also purchase additional recreational supplies. In fact, you might put the money toward that wireless-microphone set I keep whining about.

You can also hold Resident Council-sponsored auctions for specific causes like the Heart, Alzheimer's or Kidney Foundations - or for a staff member who suffered a recent tragedy like a fire or flood. We held one shortly after the 9-11 Twin Towers tragedy in 2001 and not only raised a good amount of money but gave staff and family members a chance to contribute to a worthwhile cause. In cases like this, you will probably switch to the fifty-cent or three-for-a-dollar ticket price. In fact, some people will simply donate and give their tickets to residents.

Hometown Happenings

Discussion Group

What it is:

A "Home Town Happenings" discussion group is a reminiscence group themed toward each participant's recollections of his or her hometown. It provides some great opportunities for sharing early memories and comparing the similarities and differences of the participants' backgrounds.

What you will likely need:

You won't need much preparation for this activity. There are several useful books and booklets that will help you prompt the participants in their memory treasure hunts. A few of my favorites include *Remembering the Good Old Days* and *Looking Back* by Marge Knoth; the reminiscing decade books - *The 1940's (and other decades) Remembering and Reminiscing for Seniors* by John Artman and Gary Grimm; and if you can find it in a used book Internet store, the classic *Discussion Topics for Oldsters in Nursing Homes* by Toni Merrill. They are chuck-full of memory prompters, with suggested questions in various categories.

58

For example, in a section on home remedies and early medication, you will find questions about mustard plasters, sassafras tea, "tar cloths," spring tonics and cold medicines with tasty *turpentine* (yup, they *drank* it). The questions on early school days will help the residents dredge up recollections of reciting poetry in front of the class, helping the teacher clean the blackboard erasers, one-room school houses and wild-eyed teachers wielding finger-whacking rulers. As with other reminiscing activities, antiques and vintage pictures are also great memory-ticklers.

How it looks:

This layout is a simple one. It works best with the participants in a circle and you as part of that circle. This provides everyone with a front-row seat.

What you do:

Since you will theme this group toward the participants' hometowns, you will likely want to start off with each resident telling the group where they grew up. Be sure to include yourself, so you appear to be more of an equal participant than a professional moderator. This can help loosen up residents who might feel you are putting them on the spot with your questioning. You can use a microphone and amplifier so your voice is clear to any hearing-impaired residents.

Since the conversation is going to jump from one person to the next, it is not very practical to pass the mike back and forth. Of course, being a big fan of microphones, I tried this once. You will simply need to do a little "mumble interpreting" as you go along, like - "Mary said she hated reading poems in front of the class; how about the rest of you?" Similarly, if one participant poses a question to someone who just talked, you will often need to repeat it so everyone can hear, like - "John was wondering what you paid for that Model T Ford you mentioned."

One of the best ways to link the group members together is to ask questions throughout the discussion. If someone talks about their hometown movie theater for instance, you might ask the group, "How much did movies cost when you were young?" Or if the discussion turns toward automobiles, you could inquire, "What price do you remember paying for gas in your town?" This is also a tricky way of switching the focus from the occasional conversation dominator.

Once the group gets rolling, you can often steer one conversation topic toward the next. For example, if someone is talking about a game they played with their brother, you can move into early childhood games like marbles; Hopscotch; Annie, Annie Over; Kick the Can; and jump rope. If you have a few fairly good talkers, you can often jump-start several minutes of happy recollection with the mere mention of penny candies, early radio or television shows, the price of various items when they were young or their first jobs.

Another good memory-prompting trick is to take informal *polls* such as "How many of you were born at home?" "Who had electricity when they were growing up?" "Who remembers Dinner on the Ground?" or "How many of you had an outhouse?" Let your own curiosity drive your questions and you'll not only stoke the memory furnace but also learn a lot of cool stuff yourself (especially if you are a young *whippersnapper).* As you might tell, this was always one of my favorite activities. It is worth considering as a bimonthly or quarterly event, along with regularly scheduled general reminiscence groups.

 # "The Times of Our Lives" Memory Booklet

What it is:

Creating a group memory booklet is one of those projects that takes some time, but also produces some great results. The booklet is a compilation of the residents' recollections, and can make a great thank-you gift for volunteers. I have had a number of volunteer entertainers who have kept a collection of the booklets they received throughout the years.

What you will likely need:

You'll need a method of preserving the residents' memories as they recall them. There are a couple of possible methods. You can record their stories and later transcribe them, or write them as they talk. Also, in rare cases, a family member will write down a resident's memories. If so, you might need to remind them you only need a couple paragraphs for the booklet.

My preference was to hold two *memory-sharing* groups to record the input for the booklet. If you are going to create a 16-page booklet - which makes a nice little gift-size - I would suggest creating a page thanking the writers and readers of the booklet, as well as a second page explaining the concept of the booklet. For the first page you might use a piece of clip art like a sun, heart, gift box or something similar implying that the booklet is a gift to the recipient from the resident writers. Beneath that, you might note that the booklet contains one of the greatest gifts one person can give another, *their memories*.

Your *thank you* page might look something like this:

THANK YOU!
to our volunteers who bring in the sunshine and our resident writers who shared the most valuable gift they have to give... *their memories!*

As an example of a possible second *explanation page,* here's the copy from one of our booklets:

The Briarwood "Times of Our Lives" project captures gleaming chunks of raw buried treasure. The tales are not smoothly crafted stories, but uneven slices of memories built from the sensations and experiences of life.

That is what gives them their unique value. They're pieces of lives and times painted with laughter, sorrow and all the rainbow colors of life. As you soak them in, get ready to see the world through the eyes of those who loved, laughed and cried their way through it.

The stories are nearly verbatim transcripts of the resident participants and were recorded during sessions of our *Writer's Club* meetings.

Following the *thank you* and *explanation* pages, you will have fourteen pages for the actual stories. If you gather seven stories in each group, you are *ready to roll.*

How it looks:

One thing I liked about gathering the memories during the two group sessions is that rather than taking time away from your activities, this adds to them. A circle of participants works fine, with you (or whoever is pretty fast at typing) as part of the circle. Like an old-fashioned court transcriber, that individual will try to record the residents' stories verbatim, not worrying about capitalization and punctuation. Even with a speedy keyboardist though, there will be a few times when the transcriber will have to ask a resident to "hold that thought" while catching up. There will also need to be a "roving reporter" (with a microphone if possible) interviewing each resident who agrees to share his or her memories.

What you do:

No, it is not always easy to elicit recollections for the project. In fact, most folks will begin with, "I really don't have a story to tell." With the proper mental massaging, however, they will usually come up with a unique little slice of their life that will make an ideal entry into the booklet. The reminiscing resources I mentioned for the *Hometown Happenings* discussion will also come in handy here.

The interviewer can jump from one possible topic to the next - asking about school days, games they played, medicines their parents gave them, their first job, early radio shows they enjoyed and on and on. Hopefully something will hook a memory and pull out a story. Since we are only looking for a couple paragraphs and will print it in a large-sized font, we don't need a *biography*. In fact, as with the discussion groups, we will sometimes need to wrap up a meandering tale with, "I think that will be enough to make a great story. Thank you!"

It can be heartwarming watching the more alert group members helping you coax reflections from a cognitively impaired resident. In fact, the other residents in the circle can be some of your best *interviewers*. In some cases, you will need to make a few minor clarifications in a story to make it more easily understood. The closer the written account is to the actual story, however, the more it will reflect his or her personality.

So, now that you have held a couple memory-sharing sessions and have your fourteen little stories, you are ready to create the booklet. If you'll remember, I started this section with the comment that this project will take *a little time*. Well, here's where the time comes in. You will need to format your stories on the left side of a horizontal page. The reason for placing the story on the left half of the sheet, as you might have already guessed, is that it will become one page of a folded booklet. You can experiment with the margins by typing one sentence on the sheet, printing it out, then folding the horizontal sheet in half. You will simply be using regular-sized 8 1/2 X 11-inch copy paper. This is also the time you will check the spelling and add the punctuation and capitalization. It will make it easier to compile the booklet if you add page numbers to the bottom of the fourteen stories. Each page will look something like this:

You might have noticed that I also stuck in a little piece of clip art. This takes a little more time, but adds a touch of class to the finished project. Most likely you'll be using Microsoft Word, so take advantage of the Microsoft clip art website. If you haven't used this, you should try it...not only for this but for flyers and other projects as well. You can reach their website by clicking on "insert," then "pictures," "clip art," and finally, "clips on line." When you enter a topic in the *search* function area, you will see possible pictures you can use. You don't need to worry about downloading the clipart unless you want to, but can simply copy it from the site and paste it in your project.

Once you do, you will need to format the artwork by selecting "format," then "picture," "layout," and then changing the layout to either "in front of" or "behind" the text. While you are in that section, you can change the color (under the "color" tab) to black and white or grayscale. If this is beginning to sound like a foreign language, you might need to call on a computer *geek* co-worker or family member to help walk you through the process a time or two.

The clip art will come in especially handy in creating a cover for your little booklet. Like the pages I discuss in the next few paragraphs, the front and back cover sections are most easily made from two half-page sections. Here is a sample cover

Once you have modified your fourteen stories and added the thank-you page, the explanation page and the

cover, you are ready to make master sheets to create your booklet. Incidentally, you might prefer to arrange the stories on the computer pages themselves using text boxes, but for my taste, the good old fashion *low tech* way seemed quicker. First, print all sixteen sheets out. Then take four blank sheets (you can use little scratch pad sheets to save a tree) and fold them, one inside another. Now, write "thank you" on the first page, "explanation" on the second, and number the remaining pages, "1" through "14." Incidentally, in the *printing biz*, this is known as making a "dummy."

Now, here comes the old fashion "cut & paste" part. Using your little dummy booklet as a guide, cut the sheets in half that will be placed on the right side of a page. For example, the thank-you page will be on the right side of page 14. So fold the sheet with the thank you page in half (easiest way to measure the halfway line) and cut it with scissors or a paper cutter. Then, using stick glue, paste it on the right side of the sheet that has page 14 on the left side.

Once this is completed, fold the sheet with page 13 and cut it. Then, using the stick glue, place it on the right side of the sheet with the explanation page on its left. You don't need to glue the two finished sheets together, but can just slide them back-to-back into a sheet protector. You will finish the other three front-and-back sheets in the same way. The cover will only require one cut-and-paste, since it will only have copy on the outside. I would put it in a page protector as well.

Now, take heart, you are nearly finished. You will need to create a *copy master*. Here is where you might need to do a little trial-and-error work. Place one of the finished pages on a copier and make several copies. Then, turning the master over, run the sheet you just copied through the side feeder, upside down. What you are trying to make, is a sheet with the two sides facing the same as the ones in the page protector. What you will *get* the first few times is most likely double-printed and reverse image pages that will make you go, *"What the ...!"* (hence the reason for making several copies). Once you have mastered the concept, do the same with the other three front-and-back sheets in the page protectors. The finished project is going to be your *master copy*,

So what you have now is a master copy to make as many copies of the booklet as your heart (and budget) desires. Even though it is not actually quite as complicated a process as my instructions may seem, as I said previously, it does take time. The finished booklets are also not particularly inexpensive. They will likely cost about $1.25 each for a copy shop to create a finished product - folded and stapled with a colored heavyweight cover.

On the plus side, they make the coolest *thank-you booklets* you can imagine. And they also make some resident "authors" quite proud. Also if Lady Luck is on your side, you might even be able to locate an individual or a service group that would take it on as a project. You will likely want to create a new booklet every six months...with one "publishing date" falling in November in time to give them to holiday volunteers. To whet your appetite, I have included three stories from some of my previous booklets, in the format I printed them in to give you a feel for it. You can adjust the size of the little stories by dropping the font size by one number and adding a space between the paragraphs. Of course you will want to include the name of the *author* where I wrote "name."

Back during the depression, we had a hard time and didn't have much...a place to eat and a place to stay. One Christmas, my momma took my daddy's tool chest that had a few tools in it. She took the tools out and lined the chest with pretty paper and made three Christmas cakes – chocolate, coconut and lemon cheese-cake.

My daddy came in after working with some tools and he didn't know there were cakes in the tool chest. He tossed the rusty old tools right in the middle of the beautiful cakes. It was sad because we didn't have cakes everyday. I think we salvaged part of them. We were ready to *eat the crumbs*!

(name)

My mother did not have the modern conveniences we have now. She made all the clothes we wore - but she did have a dishwasher (*mainly me*). I got so tired of washing dirty dishes that one day when she told me to take care of the dishes, I thought, "Well, *I'll show her*." We had a wood-burning stove and I took every one of those dishes and stuck them in that stove & shut the door on them.

When she came in, she looked all around the kitchen and eventually opened that oven door. "What did I tell you to do with the dishes?" she asked. "Take care of them," I said, "and *I did*." Then she said, "There's a peach tree right outside the door and there's a switch on it. I want you to get a big one." Today they call that child abuse, but then they called it *correction*.

(name)

When I was about five years old, I talked incessantly and one day my aunt and I went downtown. There were a bunch of people on the corner talking in sign language, which I'd never seen before. I asked my aunt what they were doing and she told me that "people had only so many words to say in their lives" and these people had run out of words.

Later I heard her laughing about the joke she had pulled on me. I had believed it for a number of days. It wasn't until I overheard her talking about it in the kitchen that I found out she had been joking. I had gone around for quite a while pointing and nodding to save words.

(name)

 # A Lifetime Achievement Celebration

What it is:

A Lifetime Achievement Celebration, as the name implies, focuses on the accomplishments of various residents throughout their lives. This activity developed as an alternative to organizing a facility pageant. A couple of my co-workers had been hounding me to organize a pageant. I liked the idea of residents dressing up for a classy event but have never been much for pageants in the long-term care field. They tend to focus on qualities like physical attractiveness or a sparkling personality, which, unfortunately, may have diminished throughout the years. Also, the competitive element can leave some disappointed residents since only one person will receive the main prize. So in the spirit of compromise we kept the pomp and ceremony of the pageant, but focused it toward another criteria – individual achievement and service to others.

What you will likely need:

Since such varying achievements as having served as a Girl Scout leader, winning a "Teacher of the Year" award or hosting several foster children are apples-and-oranges comparisons, there will be no winner involved in the event. Rather than presenting an award, you can make a *certificate of achievement* for each participant. If you are using a Microsoft Word word-processing program, check among the graphics on their clip-art website, for backgrounds as well as frames. There are several colorful designs that will make the finished product sparkle. If you are selecting a background, you will want one with a large open center so you can add a couple paragraphs about the resident. You can also use a photograph with a text box in front of it. Check out page 137 for more information about using photographs.

When you gather the information about the resident's accomplishments, your primary source will likely be their family members...who are usually happy to help. As you add this information to the certificate, you will be inserting a *text box* into the project. Be sure to use a fairly large-size easy-to-read font. You want the resident to be able to read it. Beginning with something like "In Appreciation of Mary Smith" (in a larger bold font) you will highlight the resident's achievements that the family told you about. For example, if the family told you Mary was a reading tutor for eighteen years, took in her nephew who later became a veterinarian and was always known for bringing the best home-baked pies to family reunions, you might come up with something like this:

IN APPRECIATION OF MARY SMITH

Mary has definitely let her *light shine* on those around her throughout her life. She didn't hesitate in taking her nephew, John, into her family when he lost his parents. His success as a local veterinarian has also spread the glow of that light to many *furry friends* around her town.

While raising her nephew and her own family, she never failed to find the time and energy to help bring the magic of reading to those she assisted during her eighteen years in the adult-education reading tutoring program. During their Christmas parties, those lucky folks also found out what her family and friends already knew - that Mary's *magical* skills also including making the world's best apple pie!

Once you have the background graphic and text box section written, you a ready to print it. Be sure, however, to save the file, since you will use it for all the other certificates. Once you've saved it (and backed up the file), simply delete the text-box input and start on the next resident's certificate. You can either save each certificate on a separate file, or save all the certificate pages on one file.

If you have a color printer in your facility, you're good to go. If not, you have a couple of options. If you are able to save the files to a flash drive, you can take it to a local copy shop and print them on their color printer. Some nursing and assisted living companies, though, work off a central computer network and have disabled the USB connection that you would need to save it to the outside flash drive. This is done, as you might suspect, to prevent someone from downloading a file that might have a hidden virus in it. If this is the case in your center, there's still another possibility. You can attach the file or files to an e-mail message you will send to your home computer. Then, at home, open the attachment, save it to a flash drive, and take that to a copy shop. You could also, of course, print it yourself and give the business office an invoice for a few dollars to compensate yourself for the ink used.

The next step is to frame the certificates and just as with the volunteer certificates, you can usually find some pretty good-looking frames at a reasonable cost. The 8 & 1/2 X 11-inch certificate frames will fit your paper size perfectly. Or if you have a little extra money rolling around in the budget barrel (not likely I suppose) you can jump up to an 11 X 14-inch size. You will need to enlarge the certificate as well.

How it looks:
You'll need a couple long tables and tablecloths at the end of the room where you will be talking. The framed certificates will be laid out there in advance. If you can

arrange for a family member to bring a picture of the resident involved in one of the activities you will be mentioning, place it near their certificate of achievement. The audience will be seated in rows of chairs and wheelchairs facing the tables.

What you do:
Obviously you can't make one of these certificates for everybody in the center. About ten or twelve seems to be a logical number of residents to honor for the event. The fairest way to select the residents to be honored is by *seniority* at your facility - starting with the earliest admission date and moving forward. We are going to want to give them to residents who will be able to read and enjoy them; so cognitive ability will be another deciding factor. You might want to schedule quarterly or semiannual Resident Achievement Celebrations in order to reach more residents as time goes on.

As I said previously, the event can have a similar atmosphere to that of a pageant, with those being honored sporting their best dresses or suits topped off with a carnation corsage or boutonniere. Be sure to invite their family members early on so they can arrange their schedule in order to attend. We had a lot of enthusiasm and good attendance from the families. In fact, make sure to ask them if they would like to say a little something about their honored resident. The actual event, like anything else, can be as classy as time and your budget allows. A piano player or other instrumentalist can add a little pomp to the activity while everybody enters, mingles and finds a seat.

After the live music (or CD if you can't find a volunteer musician), you will begin presenting the certificates. If a family member has a few words to say, let them talk...and when they are through, read the certificate to the group -

then present it to the resident. You can add a touch of flourish to the presentation if you have the individual come forward and sit in a chair or wheelchair while you read the certificate and someone takes a picture. You will likely want to sit as well when you do this, so you are not *towering* over them. You might want to put the certificate back on the table once you've read it, so they won't need to hold it the entire time. Your certificates might end up looking something like this:

After each resident has received their certificate, it is time for snacks - and perhaps a little more music to top off the event. During this time, folks might want to look at the display tables and the resident's pictures. Light refreshments will do for the snacks, and since residents will be in their finery, I would strongly suggest serving them after the presentation is completed. Punch stains don't add a lot to an evening gown.

A "Home-grown" Veteran's Day or Memorial Day Event

What it is:

A "home-grown" Veteran's Day or Memorial Day event, like the name implies, is a commemoration of either day – which doesn't rely on outside organizations. It can sometimes make more of a personal impact than a formalized presentation by a community organization. In fact, this concept developed as a fallback activity when planning fell through for a formal VFW presentation for a Veteran's Day activity.

What you will likely need:

You are certain to have a number of residents, family members and staff who have served in the armed forces. If you can interest a few of them in giving a brief talk about their experiences, you have the basis of an exceptionally meaningful activity.

Let them know that you don't expect a professional presentation and that there will be other speakers there as well. If they have any pictures of their fellow soldiers, airplane, ship and such - all the better. From experience, I have found that although some folks will not be interested, several *will be.* As with other projects that require participation from staff, family members or volunteers, posters and announcement won't cut it alone. Nothing trumps face-to-face contact.

How it looks:

Usually an informal setting like a circle of residents

works best, so the presenters can easily walk around showing their pictures or memorabilia. You might also schedule an assistant or volunteer to show the pictures and objects around while you interview the presenter.

What you do:

You only need a few presenters for a successful event. Even the quiet ones will often blossom out when they begin talking about their military experiences. Some folks will have photos and other display items related to their own service. Even if veterans don't have anything specific to show, you can give them presentation tools printed from the Internet that can include them in the event. Providing them with copies of some military-related trivia questions, historical military facts, or patriotic poems, can help them become a meaningful part of the activity.

After the speakers give their presentations, you can ask each resident to honor anyone in their family who served in the armed forces. Then you can top it off with a couple of patriotic poems like In Flanders Fields or The Flag Goes By. Add some CDs or DVDs of patriotic songs like Johnny Cash's *Ragged Old flag*, Lee Greenwood's *Proud to be an American*, Elvis's *American Trilogy* and Kate Smith's *God Bless America* and you've got yourself a Veteran's Day event that will leave lasting memories.

One year, a family member reluctantly agreed to participate in the event. I had a feeling, though, that he was actually looking forward to the activity, since he asked several related questions during the weeks preceding it. Besides, his sister was our resident and had also served in the military. Sure enough, when the time came, he showed up with a typed presentation and a number of pictures of his and his sister's military experiences neatly labeled and enclosed in page protectors. In addition, he was decked out in his old Army uniform (a tad snug, but looking great).

A Personalized Thank you Certificate

What it is:

This project is a resident-signed thank you certificate or card that can mean a lot more to a volunteer than the standard version.

What you will likely need:

There are a number of eye-catching greeting cards available with a blank interior. On the left side, you can write a line or two like, "Thank you Brownie Troop 345 for bringing the sunshine in with your musical presentation - from all your friends at ABC Nursing Center. At an activity prior to their appearance, pass the card around for residents to sign on the right interior and back. If there is no table in the activity to place the card on, you can use an over-bed table.

Similarly, you can create a personalized thank-you certificate that will make the classiest gold-trimmed version pale in comparison. If your facility doesn't have one, you might be able to sweet talk administration into springing for a color printer. In fact, you might be able to join forces in your sweet-talking campaign, with the in-service director, since full-color flyers and posters will perk up training material and meeting announcements.

If you don't have a color printer and your campaign falls through, you can class up a black-and-white certificate by printing it on the colored-design copy paper available at office supply stores. First, create a page-sized certificate on a computer and save it in a file (and back it up in another in case you mess up and delete it).

A graphic border and a clip-art illustration will give you the basic certificate. In a similar manner to the thank-you card, you will type in a personal note near the top of the certificate, ending it with...from all your friends at ABC Nursing Center.

How it looks:
Maybe something like this:

What you do:
Once the residents have signed the certificate, you can put it in an inexpensive frame (the dollar-store frames aren't all that bad) and present it after their performance or service. The card or certificate with the shaky signatures will often go straight to the heart, since it came straight from the residents.

You might also want to have a certificate created in another file that fills the entire page with the wording and a background design. This can come in handy if you have a surprise visit, such as the children's choir of a regularly scheduled church group during the holiday season. You can quietly slip out of the performance for a moment...run to your computer and call up the file. In a couple minutes you can type the name of the group into the pre-made certificate, maybe throw in a related piece of clip art, and print it out. Then slap it in a dollar-store frame and waltz calmly back into to the group. When you present it at the end of their performance with an *aw shucks, it was nothin'* attitude, you will look like an activity magician.

It might look something like this:

Resident and Staff "Spotlight" Display

What it is:

A resident and staff "Spotlight" display focuses on their past accomplishments. This wall display is usually located in a prominent area of the facility and can be as extensive as time and energy allow. It can be as simple as hanging four 11x14-inch picture frames with a little explanation of the display in the middle.

What you will likely need:

Two of the frames would contain two or three early pictures of two different residents and two would display pictures of two staff members. You will probably want to make photocopies of the actual pictures. They can be trimmed and attached with stick glue, to a sheet of dark-colored poster board as a background.

A small write-up in the frame provides a mini-biography of the individual. This doesn't need to be more than a couple paragraphs highlighting the individual's background, including their hometown, childhood memories, military and work experience, family life and so forth. You might want to make a little list of questions to ask when you are gathering this input.

Questions like "What is your favorite memory of your mother or father?" "What was your favorite childhood game or activity?" "Who was your favorite (or least favorite) teacher?" "Where did you meet your spouse?" "What is the funniest thing your children ever did?" and "What advice would you have for younger people starting out in life?" tend to get some interesting responses. If a resident is unable to tell you the information, a family member might be interested in helping out. One reason you only need a short write-up is that you will want to print it in a large easy-to-read type. A bold 14 or 16-point sans serif (no little "feet") font like *Arial* seems to stand out well.

How it looks:

Here's an example of a Spotlight collage: The pictures glued on the dark blue or black poster board background give it a little of the appearance of a matted collage.

What you do:

It would be great if you could make one of these displays for every resident and staff member in the building but as you know, you have a few other balls to juggle...like *running an activity program.* You might occasionally luck out and find a volunteer or service organization that would take on the project. The display will rotate - once again, as often as time and energy allow. The most logical way to select the individuals you will be highlighting is by seniority of employment or admission date. That way you can easily explain why "mamma hasn't been up on the wall yet."

A Coffee-house Party

What it is:

A Coffeehouse party features various flavors of coffee as well as appropriate entertainment. It can be programmed either as a separate event or a theme for a monthly birthday party.

What you will likely need:

The instant coffee mixes, like Maxwell House International Café work well for this and actually taste pretty good. Two or three different flavors such as French Vanilla, Suisse Mocha and Hazelnut give the residents a choice and a little bit of the coffeehouse feeling. You will most likely want a sugar-free coffee mix, which is usually in the same section as the others. Both the French Vanilla and Suisse Mocha come in a sugar-free version. Snack cookies are logical companions to the coffee - especially the ones from other countries. Most grocery stores have a small section of international cookies like the English Carr's ginger lemon crèmes and *Walker's* shortbread raspberry; Danish *Royal Dansk* butter cookies and Belgian's *Delacre* chocolate cookies and biscuits. As you might expect, they are more costly than most, so you might just include a couple of foreign selections and "pad" the rest of the serving plate with old standards like sugar wafers and Oreos.

A couple of movable carts work well for serving the coffee and snacks. Since you will likely schedule the event between lunch and dinner, you might be able to borrow them from the dietary department. Hopefully the dietary folks can also let you use a couple of large coffee thermos containers. Usually they use these for serving the coffee on the wings or units. You'll want them rinsed out and filled with hot water (cooled off a bit so nobody gets burned). If you are successful in obtaining the carts and hot water containers, you are ready to roll.

How it looks:

As with any other party, lack of space will be your mortal enemy. If possible, you will want to try to leave room for a small wheeled-cart (or two) to carry the snacks to the tables. Although you can make do by mixing the coffees on a table by the wall, it works a little more smoothly if you can wheel right up to the table. Other than that, the layout is typical *party style*...slightly-organized chaos.

What you do:

Twelve-ounce Styrofoam cups will fill the bill for the coffee. Just follow the directions on the instant coffeehouse coffee cans. Usually three rounded teaspoons will make a good cup of coffee. It mixes easier if you scoop in the mixture, add a half cup of hot water, mix it well - then add the rest of the water and stir it again. If you want to add a touch of class, squirt a dab of whipped cream on top and maybe even add a touch of cinnamon or a few chocolate sprinkles.

The entertainment for the event should fit the coffeehouse atmosphere. Singer/songwriters are a good match. Local music shops and school music departments might be able to put you in touch with someone who would enjoy the opportunity to sing to an audience. If you can swing it, you might want to offer a small donation or gift. You might also want to contact a nearby writers' club and invite two or three local poets to read their work. A little donation would be nice here too, but most writers would love the idea of having some appreciating ears to hear their poems. There was a great cartoon in the *Writers' Digest* magazine a few years back. A man was sitting in the front of an airplane he had obviously just hijacked, holding a gun in one hand and a book in the other. "Don't worry," he declared, "If nobody moves, no one will get hurt. I just want to read you some of my poetry!"

 # A "Turn-the-Tables" Volunteer Appreciation

What it is:

Since our volunteers spend the rest of the year helping us provide activities for the residents, this appreciation event can *turn the tables* and let them participate in their own "activities." It consists of a casual Volunteer Appreciation along with a horserace or Bingo game, and can sometimes outshine a more expensive sit-down dinner and reception. You can give them a taste of the fun that their activities are providing to the residents. I know this concept might sound a little strange, but I have had some real success with our old standbys - good old Racemania and Bingo.

What you will likely need and how it looks:

Now, remember that we're going to end up with a group activity for the volunteers, so this appreciation event will have an unusual layout. If you'll be playing Bingo, the volunteers and residents will be seated around tables. If it is *Racemania*, they will be in semicircular rows facing the racing table. The reason for using more than one row, as you might imagine, is that your little activity or dining room will likely be busting at the seams. In fact, you might want to get word out to staff that due to space restrictions, not every resident in the building can participate. Of course if you have enough room, everybody is welcome.

Your Resident Council president and vice president (or co-presidents) should definitely be there, as well as maybe about a dozen "council representatives." You might want to ask in advance for residents who particularly want to attend. Explain to the others that you are only keeping the resident number relatively low so there will be plenty of room for the volunteers to find seats for the event. If you are truly pushed for room, you might have to settle for only the volunteers but I would suggest trying to squeeze in as many residents as possible, since *they* are the ones the volunteers are actually working for.

What you do:

Here's a suggested schedule if you want to give this idea a try. If you have developed a resident chorus or bell ringer group, let them start the event off with a brief concert for the volunteers. Even if you don't have a formalized group, you can always play two or three old-time Karaoke CD songs like "You Are My Sunshine," "Let Me Call You Sweetheart" and "I'll Be Loving You." The company, Sound Choice, has developed a reminiscence CD series that has both vocal and non-vocal versions of old standards. You will probably want to use the vocal version to give a little assistance to their concert. Be sure to point out to the volunteers that the sentiments in the songs express the residents' feelings toward them.

Next, you might want to move right to refreshments. Of course snacks are an expected part of the event but for this type of informal activity, finger foods and fancy cookies and crackers are sufficient. In fact since we're really combining an appreciation with a volunteer-oriented activity, there is no real expectation of fancy tablecloths and silverware. Decorator paper plates and matching napkins fill the bill for the cookies and snacks. In fact, for the drinks, you might consider using small pre-chilled bottles of soda because they are less likely to mess up the event than tumbling ice tea and lemonade glasses. Just let the volunteers know that the reason for the finger food and mini soda bottles is that the program will soon be getting "wild and crazy." Once everyone is peacefully munching away, you can begin the appreciation part of the event.

As the various volunteers are highlighted, they can stand and talk a little bit about their volunteer functions and how long they are been giving their service. Then, they can receive a keepsake gift from the Resident Council officers. Something like a miniature picture of the residents (with their permission of course) in a refrigerator frame or in an inexpensive photo-frame Christmas ornament can mean more than an expensive generic volunteer gift. The photo-ornaments are available from *Oriental Trading* catalogs in bulk orders at pretty reasonable prices. It is, of course, up to you whether you introduce each volunteer or have them introduce themselves. Unless you have a steel-trap memory, you might want to let them do it and avoid potentially embarrassing memory lapses or mispronunciations of their names.

Start with someone you are very familiar with and introduce them and give a brief overview of their volunteer history, like..."We'll start with Roger Autry, our sing-a-long leader. He has been with us for three years and the residents always look forward to his lively singing and piano playing during his monthly visits." (Of course, each volunteer will get a round of applause in turn). Then Roger will go to the council representatives and receive his keepsake gift and return to his seat. You might then say, "Now, let's go around the room and let everyone know who you are, what you do and how long you've been doing it. If you would, please try to speak loudly so we can all hear." This can also be a method of avoiding the ego-crushing situation we have all witnessed at similar functions of, "Now have we recognized everyone? Oh, I'm *so sorry* Barbara..."

Once everyone has been recognized and has received their keepsake, it is time for the *games to begin*. Of course the resident attendees will also participate but the volunteers are the primary focus. If you are using Bingo as your game, I would suggest playing straight through rather than clearing the cards. As the residents win, they will get quarters or whatever you traditionally give. When a volunteer wins, however, they can take a trip to a prize table, filled with dollar store-type gift items.

If you are going the *Racemania* route, three games seem to be an ideal amount, with two winning numbers for the first two races and three on the last one. Keeping with the volunteer focus, they will select the names for the horses (or whatever racers you use) and do most of the throwing of the die. Once again, residents get their traditional prize and volunteers head to the prize table. As you have likely already noticed, you can get some pretty neat little goodies at a dollar store. If your budget can swing it, make sure you have more than enough game prizes for all the volunteers. Those who didn't win during the games can select a prize after the last game.

I know this volunteer appreciation concept is a little more laid back than traditional functions, but I've had some great reviews from the volunteers who attended. It's fun to see the normally subdued Bible-study leaders or piano players shouting a heartfelt "Bingo" or whooping and hollering for their horse to cross the finish line.

A Bag of
"Tricks or Tweaks"

And now, here's a sprinkling of miscellaneous time-tested programs and projects.   Many of these entries are *tweaks* that can add a novel touch to traditional groups. Some are *tricks*-of-the-trade for the *newbies* who may not have run across them yet.

A ***wedding photograph display*** is a twist on the Life and Times display. It is planned and carried out in exactly the same manner. If anyone is concerned about bringing in their original wedding photo, they can make a photocopy. The display is open to residents, staff, volunteers and family members. Later, you can frame the copied pictures with labels, to create wall displays like this one:

A ***poetry corner*** reading group can renew interest in some of the classic poems the residents grew up with. This activity definitely requires a microphone and amplifier. As I mentioned in the introduction, a poetry-reading activity makes a good half-hour group. As you read familiar poems like Joyce Kilmer's *Trees* or Ernest Lawrence Thayer's *Casey at the Bat*, you will likely see some residents mouthing the words along with you. Many of them memorized the poems in school. There's a side benefit to this activity as well. If you don't already enjoy poetry, you may find yourself developing an appreciation for it. My favorite resource is *Poetry for a Lifetime* by Samuel Etheredge.

An ***antique car display*** will definitely get most of the guys involved. What you will be snooping around for is a local antique car club with a few members who wouldn't mind bringing over their cars for an hour or so. A great place to fish for volunteers is at a car show in a festival or fair. Now and then you might run across one in a shopping center parking lot. Many of the participants will belong to clubs of various kinds, like a Model A club or a Corvette club. You might also luck out as I once did, with a personal connection. One of our resident's husbands was a member of the local Model A club and talked the group into providing a display of their wonderful classic vehicles in our parking lot.

A **karate demonstration** is an attention-getter that gives your residents a lively spectacle to enjoy. This one's an easy one to line up. Just give local Karate clubs a call. The instructors are often happy to be able to show off their class and the students get a "kick" out of breaking boards in front of an audience. A framed resident-signed certificate like the one I talked about previously, makes a great thank you, since they can hang it in their Karate *dojo*.

Another popular performance is a ***juggling exhibition***. Unlike the Karate class, you'll most likely have to pay for this one. If you are in or near a fairly large town, you probably have a professional juggler available. They often perform at children's birthday parties. You will need a fairly large space, especially if they bring a unicycle. A juggler makes an ideal performer for a Grandparent's Day celebration in which you've invited their grandkids for a special event. A professional magician (also a kid's birthday party entertainer) makes a perfect performer for that type of program as well.

A *flower show* is a colorful event that brings back warm memories to the gardeners in your center. As with most displays, it is open to residents, volunteers and family and staff members. You might also contact local clubs like 4-H and garden groups. Once again, I would suggest holding a *show* rather than a *contest*. If you set up the room in a similar fashion to the other shows I've mentioned, with walking room between the rows of chairs or wheelchairs, one person can walk up and down with the flower while the other talks to the individual who provided it. Since the majority of your residents were probably gardeners of some variety, this group will very likely catch their interest.

And now, here are a few thoughts about *intergenerational activities.* They are, of course, especially important to residents whose children and grandchildren may live out of the area. Scheduling regular visits by daycare and elementary classes is more difficult than it once was due to insurance concerns and school regulations. One alternative is to contact the parents of home-schooled children. They have often formed social groups with other home-schooled families to help their children maintain regular school-based friendships. Also, scout troops of all varieties are ideal for intergenerational programming.

There are two basic structures to these visits. In a traditional "Adopt-a-Grandparent" setting, each child will be paired with a particular resident. In a less structured *group-adopt-a-group* type of format, there will still be bonding between individuals but with no formalized pairing. From experience, the latter is usually more practical. Even with the best of intentions, young people in a group who commit to regularly scheduled visits are bombarded with other responsibilities and activities. Soccer, football and cheerleading practice can gobble up their scheduled visiting times. This can lead to some very disappointed residents. The rare child who is actually able to maintain a regular visiting schedule can do that outside of the group visits.

Children's groups are naturals for pumping spirit into the holidays. A group of daycare kids singing "Itsy Bitsy Spider," "Little Bunny Foo Foo" or "Away in a Manger" can often top your best-planned high-budget holiday parties. Also, as I mentioned before, scout troops or home-schooled groups make excellent additions to reminiscing sessions - especially those involving antiques and collectibles. Quart milk bottles, sad irons, ink wells, shaving mugs & brushes and similar objects might have faded into history but remain vivid memories for many of the residents. They can present a colorful *living history* lesson for the children...which is exactly the way it should be - the older people teaching the young.

Speaking of Living History, **_educational presentations and lectures_** furnish intellectual stimulation that will attract a number of the higher cognitive-level residents. Local writers, travelers, artists and collectors might be coerced into coming in to talk about their interests and accomplishments. Through the years, I have witnessed some great resident response to this type of activity. Potential presenters, in fact, are sometimes lurking among the family and staff members. They don't need to be experts; just passionate about their area of interest. For instance, one resident's daughter kept the female residents' attention riveted as she discussed and displayed her collection of antique dolls. As you might imagine, she elicited choruses of "I had one just like that!" And similarly, the guys were transfixed as a resident's retired history-professor husband gave an audio-visual show on the people and events of the Old West along the Overland Trail.

This one is a sure-fire _ooh_ and _aah_ producer. Churches will sometimes organize **_puppet shows_** for the young people in their congregation to take out on the road. If you are fortunate enough to have one in your area, be sure to try to sweet talk them into performing for your center. The residents, _and you_, will love it. Often the church's men's club will make the puppet theater while the ladies organization creates the hand puppets and marionettes for the kids to operate. Speaking of churches, while you are calling around for puppet shows and such, don't forget to ask the music minister about choruses and gospel quartets that might come over. In the past, I know some activity programs have been too heavily weighted with religious programming...to the point that their activity calendars began to look more like *church calendars*, but special presentations by a local church chorus or quartet, remain some of the most popular offerings we can arrange.

A ***folk-dancing performance*** provides a very colorful and entertaining event. If you are in or near a relatively large city, you might be lucky enough to have access to some folk-dancing clubs. The dancers will usually dress in the outfits of the country or countries whose dances they are performing, and give some information about the origin of the various dances. Even if they charge a nominal fee or donation for their traveling expenses, this type of activity is a memorable event usually well worth the money.

Hosting a club meeting of an organization that a resident previously belonged to, can keep them in touch with their friends. Just because he or she can no longer attend the outside meetings doesn't mean that connection needs to end. Obviously if the group will be using the activity area, the meeting should be scheduled either before or after group activities. Usually you will only need to set up an area with a few chairs and maybe a pitcher of ice water and glasses. The club members can handle the rest.

A *spring or fall festival* can be a lot of fun (and, of course, a lot of work). Modeled after the festivals that schools or community groups hold, the event can consist of serving snack foods like popcorn, snow cones, cotton candy and such as well as organizing various games - usually targeted for children. Something of this kind works best as an interdepartmental undertaking, maybe for Grandparent's Day or National Nursing Home or Assisted Living celebrations.

The games can be run by residents, volunteers and staff members and often include carnival-type skill games like ring toss, a light-weight basketball throw, golf-putting and a bean-bag toss. A balloon-animal maker adds a festive touch. Toss in some lively music, face-painting, colorful decorations, a couple of jelly bean-guessing jars and maybe a hula hoop contest and you've whipped up something that should entertain the kids and grandkids of the residents, staff and community members on a Saturday afternoon, in good fashion. If you are like most and are not blessed with spacious activity areas, you will need to either pray for a sunny day and take it outside or squeeze it between lunch and dinner in the dining room.

A ***resident-run garden*** can bring back fond memories of "playing in the dirt" for many folks. There are a number of ready-made wheelchair garden boxes as well as plans to make them. Just search the Internet and you'll run across both. This is one of those projects that can be as extensive as time, energy and your budget permits. You might keep the wheelchair garden box (or boxes) concept in mind for the next time a service organization or Eagle Scout inquires about a possible project. The boxes need to be heavily constructed to hold the soil and sand or gravel involved. A garden club would be an ideal resource to tap for volunteers to come over and help the residents take care of their box-gardens. Our "Bloom Buggy" (since it was on wheels) was a pretty popular project.

Of course, even if you don't have an outside garden area, you can still provide some of the enjoyment of growing flowers or vegetables, through gardening groups. The residents can plant seeds and bulbs in pots to place in the activity area windowsills or on plant stands in common areas or in their rooms. Flower-arranging groups will also interest the *green thumbs* in the center. Sometimes you might want to schedule an impromptu flower-arranging group to create attractive vases of fresh flowers for areas in the facility...out of the funeral arrangements family members often drop off after a funeral. Unfortunately, the arrangements usually look like exactly what they are - *funeral flowers*, and can seem a little less than upbeat in a nursing center.

This is one of those *old standby* activities I wanted to mention for the newcomers to our field. Working a **group crossword puzzle** is not only an enjoyable activity, but helps to keep the gray matter flowing. Suppliers like S & S and Nasco have several varieties of large-size crossword puzzles. These can be taped onto a sturdy backing and mounted on an easel. Dark-colored wide-tipped markers will make nice clear letters.

Even with the large puzzles and markers, however, some residents are not going to be able to make out the letters on their own. After you read the clue from the sheet, you must usually give some verbal help, like "This is going to be a five-letter word going across. We already have the first two letters - a "B" and an "L"...then two blank spaces, and we know it ends with a "K." Even though we are giving a little help to assist them in visualizing the puzzle, we need to remember that it is *supposed* to be challenging. We don't need to quickly give extra clues if no one immediately guesses the word. We can always help fill in a horizontal word by moving on to vertical words that intersect it, and visa versa. There is nothing wrong with pausing to let residents guess at possible words. As any *puzzler* knows, the fun of working a crossword puzzle is not simply filling out the puzzle, but in solving the challenges along the way.

A **wall-mounted museum-type display** like the one on the next page, can give residents, staff and visitors a glimpse back into earlier times.

This particular one was made from an antique museum display case that was given to me by a family member who was a curator of a museum. But a large shadowbox (available at craft stores like Michaels or Hobby Lobby) also makes an ideal display case. Relatively inexpensive antiques and collectibles like those I mentioned previously in the Music and Memories presentation make a fascinating display.

Many of the shadowbox display cases come with a removable black velour backing. Small objects like old medicine bottles, tobacco tins, needle packets, war ration coupons, early presidential pins and souvenir postcards & keepsakes are all great memory starters. The heavier items like the bottles, tins and keepsakes can be attached to the backing by wrapping monofilament plastic fishing line around narrow areas or corners and sewing them to the backing sheet. The lighter items can be attached with archival quality removable adhesive dots. A small label under or beside each item identifies it and its use. Make sure the shadow box is mounted solidly to the wall when you are through. If you decide to create one, you will likely be surprised how many folks will stop by to enjoy it. You might also keep this project in mind for an Eagle Scout, who could make several throughout the facility.

An *in-house resident volunteer club* can present a win-win situation for the resident volunteers as well as the people they help. Even though people live in an assisted living or nursing center, their volunteer functions in the community can remain strong. This *community* of course, can include either their previous ones or their new *inside* community. Forming a resident volunteer club helps to formalize their efforts. One great use of the club can be to schedule in-room visiting with fellow residents. From experience, it seems that pairing two resident volunteers to visit with a reclusive or room-bound individual gives the volunteers a little moral support and helps to spur conversation. You might provide them with reminiscence picture cards like those I discuss on page 133.

Likely several of the residents have previously visited homebound community or church members in the past. Basically, that is exactly what they are continuing to do - visiting their neighbors for a little chat. This concept has been given various names throughout the years like a Resident-Helping-Resident project or a Forget-Me-Not club. Often the best time to schedule these little visits is after a group activity. As you help folks return to their rooms, you can suggest that anyone interested in doing a little friendly visiting can team up with a friend and you can take them to the room of an individual in need of a little company. You will keep track of these individual visits on your attendance records.

A resident-volunteer club can also welcome newly admitted residents and help ease the transition to their new environment. Nothing is much more comforting in a strange and scary situation than talking to someone who has gone through it and seems to be doing well. With a little help from you and the social service director, they can also acknowledge birthdays with a resident-signed card and a Happy Birthday song. Similarly, they can send get-well cards to those in the hospital. As you know, projects like these are not "busy work" designed to make the volunteers feel good about themselves. They are meaningful and much-appreciated functions.

These efforts in fact, don't even need to stop with other residents. If the group is interested and able, they can also perform volunteer functions for staff members by sending out congratulatory cards for weddings, graduations and other milestone events in their families. They might even host a little graduation party for the children of the associates. Events like this help develop a feeling of community. As another example of building this feeling, we held a fundraiser (a raffle auction, in fact) to raise money for little stocking-stuffer gifts that the resident council members gave to the associates' children and grandchildren. As you might imagine, there were some heartfelt hugs involved.

As most of us have discovered, resident volunteers can often be very helpful with the group activities as well. Nearly everyone wants to feel useful and important. Even as our abilities decline, this need doesn't go away. So if we politely turn down an offer by a resident to help gather bingo cards, stack game chips or help straighten the craft table, we are often missing a chance to give that resident a little dose of self esteem...and ourselves a *much-needed hand.*

A *"Super-large"* activity calendar with clip-art and 30 to 36-point lettering can make your activities stand out. I know it will sound huge if you've never seen one, but a wall calendar big enough to display an 8 1/2 X 11" horizontal page for each day, will not only let you create a separate sheet for every day, but allow you to use a large-sized font and add some eye-catching clip-art pictures. As you can see from the potential calendar sheet below, it does tend to jump out at you.

Friday, April 6

10:45 POETRY CORNER
11:15 NAME THAT TUNE
2:30 RACEMANIA
4:00 A TOUCH OF TRIVIA

If you decide to do this, the most practical method, from my experience, is to first create a small calendar and later *copy* and *paste* from the file you created it on - to page-sized daily calendar sheets (more about that in a bit). For a backing, you will need corkboard - which comes in rolls at office and school supply stores - as well as strips of flat molding to frame it with. The calendar backing will be attached to a wall in a high-traffic area of the center (after checking with your *powers that be* of course). As you might imagine, this would make a wonderful project for a super-nice maintenance man, spouse, teenager and his or her friends or a scout troop.

In order to calculate the dimensions you will use, you'll need to decide whether you plan to have a small space between each page of the calendar. I've seen a couple calendar backings made with a quarter-inch strip of black tape separating the sheets, which looked pretty sharp. If you will post the sheets with no space between them, the dimensions will be 6' 5" long (horizontally) by 3' 6 ½" wide (if you will have five rows) or 4' 3" if you want six rows. Some months, as you likely know, will fill six rows, if only by one or two days on either end. If you will use the black tape separation, just add the additional space into the measurement. Also, remember these dimensions will be for the *interior* of the molding frame.

So, if you've decided to try this concept and have conned someone into putting up the framed corkboard backing, you're ready to post a calendar that will have a couple of important advantages. First, each day's section will be large enough to write the activities in bold easy-to-read type, and secondly, when you add or postpone an activity later in the month, you can simply print out the new daily sheet and staple it onto the corkboard backing.

This will give you a feeling of flexibility to modify the calendar as needed during the month. This is not to say you should *shake up* the schedule too much, but there's no reason to feel you can't add a group or change a date just because your monthly schedule is finished. You will want to add a note to your monthly calendar and/or newsletter to let readers know that it would be a good idea for a family member to call you before driving in for a particular special event, since the wall calendar and not the newsletter, is always the *final* calendar.

The pages will be laid out horizontally and can be saved in a file for each day of the week. In other words, all the Monday calendars will be saved under one file; Tuesdays under another and so on. As I suggested earlier, it seems to save a little time to copy and paste changes from your smaller calendar. The reason I said *changes* is that some pages will remain nearly or entirely the same, due to repetitive weekly programming. You can copy sections by calling up both files and minimizing each in turn as you copy and then paste. Since you are going to begin with the small calendar, you will need to enlarge the font size after you have pasted it. If you average three or four groups daily, a 36-point bold font seems about right. If you have more daily groups, you'll need to experiment with the font size.

As I mentioned previously, graphics are great attention-getters - especially if you have access to a color printer. You can insert clip-art pictures by using the same method I discussed in the Times of Our Lives memory booklet section on pages 65 & 66. Since you obviously are not in the clip-art calendar-making business and have a bushel full of other duties, you will not be inserting all-new pictures every month but only changing out a few to give a fresh look to the next month's calendar. And yes, to be perfectly honest, this project will add some time to your calendar preparation. It does, however, have some pretty worthwhile benefits, so you might want to consider it.

Video games can add variety and interest to your schedule. They will all need a little *tweaking* to turn them into usable group activities. Three that I've had success with are Wheel of Fortune, Family Feud and Deal or No

Deal. With all of these, you will likely want to select the "solo game" or "single player" option and have the entire group play as one team against a competing *target score*. This score is something you will calculate after averaging a few games they've played. Your group may differ, but we usually played two games of Deal or No Deal; three of Wheel of Fortune or ten rounds of Family Feud. This will likely also vary depending upon which version you use.

We used the DVD Family Feud *3rd Edition, 2K Play* version of Deal or No Deal and the Wheel of Fortune game by *Hasbro Interactive*. Once you calculate the average score for your residents, you might want to shave off that number a little to use as the target score, in order to give them a better chance of success in future games.

You will need to pause the games fairly often, since our crowd doesn't normally have the speed the games are set for. Most of the games, however, do have time adjustments that can be modified to give you a little more leeway. In all three types of games, the residents would be in a semicircle (or rows if needed) facing a large-screen television. If you use rows, you will want to leave room between them for you and your assistant or a volunteer to walk in back of the residents to assist them if needed, in making their bids and guesses.

Various versions of the games can be purchased at good prices on Internet auction sites. The instructions for using the game will be included and, like anything else that's a tad foreign to you (unless you are a veteran video game player) you will need to do a few practice runs before you use it with residents. You will likely want to use a dry-erase board or pad on an easel to record the resident's guesses on Family Feud, while you pause the DVD.

Since all the participants are playing as one team against a predetermined target score, they will either all win or all lose. As I suggested previously, you might want to keep that score fairly low so they will usually all win. When they do, Honey Buns, Moon Pies, small sacks of Cheetos or chips, crackers, snack cakes and such can serve as the *spoils of their victory*. If they don't occasionally lose, however, the wins are going to lose their impact. When they fall short of the target score, they will get booby prizes. In our case, we said that if they won, they would get a trip to *Honey Bun Heaven*; but if they lost, they would walk the dark lonely streets of *Dum Dum City*. Yes, I know it's corny, but sometimes corny can be fun. Handing out the little Dum Dum suckers took a bit of the sting out of their loss.

A *Grandmother or Grandfather's Memory Sheet* can make a great Christmas or Birthday present to a grandchild or great-grandchild. It is a simplified version of the Grandparent's Books that you can find in bookstores. This concept makes an excellent volunteer project for teenagers, either individually or in organizations.

Since most young people are pretty computer proficient, they can gather the information at the facility and create the finished page at home on their computers. If two or more friends take on the project, it can become an enjoyable after-school volunteer function. The pages are more eye-catching if the volunteer adds a little clip art to perk it up. They might even borrow an early picture from the resident, scan it and add it to the page.

To produce the body of the little "mini-biography" you will want to create an interview form for the volunteers to use. You might include questions like: What games did you play when you were younger? What was your favorite subject in school? What was the silliest thing you can remember doing? What do you remember most about your mother and father? What accomplishment are you most proud of? What hobbies did you enjoy most? What kind of medicines do you remember taking, and which was your least favorite? What was your first job, and how much did it pay? What were your favorite radio and television shows? and What advice would you give to young people today?

The volunteers can turn the resident's answers into a brief story, using relatively large type. Since the volunteers are recording answers that the residents gave to their questions, they might want to write the little story in a first-person format, like, "I remember when my sister, Janie, used to tease me about my freckles. One night while she was asleep, I used a brown magic marker to give her freckles too. When my mother woke up, she didn't see the humor in it." After the volunteer adds a clip-art illustration or two, he or she can print the sheet to bring in for the resident. Not only will the residents end up with great memory pages they can copy and give to their grandkids, but the young volunteers who helped them will encounter some great *living history* as well.

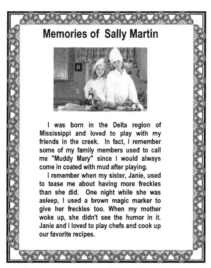

Memories of Sally Martin

I was born in the Delta region of Mississippi and loved to play with my friends in the creek. In fact, I remember some of my family members used to call me "Muddy Mary" since I would always come in coated with mud after playing.

I remember when my sister, Janie, used to tease me about having more freckles than she did. One night while she was asleep, I used a brown magic marker to give her freckles too. When my mother woke up, she didn't see the humor in it. Janie and I loved to play chefs and cook up our favorite recipes.

The memory sheets are scaled-down inside versions of the Foxfire project, where students interviewed older people in Rabun Gap, Georgia in the Appalachian mountain region. Like that project, it's a wonderful way to share one of the most valuable things people have to give...their memories. The sheet might look something like the one on the previous page.

An open-attendance **table-games group** can be a good way to program several small groupings of two or three players into a large-group setting. The participants play a variety of games simultaneously at various tables. From experience, especially in a nursing home setting, a staff member or volunteer will want to be at each table, either playing or helping keep things going (and occasionally *keeping the peace*). Dominoes and simple card and board games (as long as they are not too childish) work well in this type of mixed-game group. Of course, snacks are always welcome, just as they would be if someone invited their neighbors in for a game night.

One card game that works well with this activity is called *Shut the Box*. It is a simple game that has proven its worth through the years. Each player is given ten number cards of the same suit - face up, from the ace through the 10. The players take turns rolling a pair of dice to decide which cards to "shut" (turn over). In other words, if the player rolls a seven, he or she could turn over either the seven, a six and an ace, a three and a four, a five and a two and so forth.

The round is over when one player has "shut the box," (turned over all ten of his cards). Then a scorekeeper tallies the numbers of the cards left face up for each other player. The ace will only count one point since it is serving as a *one*. The players will decide in advance, how many rounds to play, and the overall winner is the one with the lowest score.

There are a couple of features of this game that make it successful in assisted living and nursing home environments. For one thing, the participants don't need to hold the cards in their hand or a cardholder. Also, since the cards are face up, another player or supervising staff member can make gentle suggestions like, "Let's see, you can either turn over your nine, your three and the six or your four and the five. Which do you feel is best?" This will give them some decision-making power even if they are having trouble adding the numbers.

And now, here are a few *hints for the holidays*. **Mini-pumpkin jack-o-lantern-making** is tailor made for an intergenerational activity. After a visiting group of children marches around displaying their Halloween costumes and collecting goodies, you can head them toward an area with tables, to create their miniature Jack-o-lanterns with the residents.

Together, they can draw eyes, smiles, noses and such on the little pumpkins (actually miniature gourds) with markers. Water-based markers don't work for "pumpkin art," so you will likely want to use something like the ultra fine-point Sharpie markers. You can usually find the little gourds for about a buck a piece in roadside stands or grocery stores. The kids, of course, can take their newly made treasure home and the residents can display them in their rooms. From experience, you don't want to buy them too far ahead since they *will rot.*

Easter is also a natural season for children's' groups to come over and visit. A ***combined Easter egg-dying and egg hunt*** activity can give the residents some of the pleasure they once experienced while watching their grandkids celebrate the holiday. Keep in mind though, that unless you want the housekeeping staff to make frown-faces at you for some time to come, you need to cover the tables with plastic tablecloths. In addition, you will want to have a staff member, volunteer or parent stationed at each table with a batch of paper towels and *quick reflexes.*

You will need cups for the dye and plastic spoons for the eggs. As you have likely discovered as a child, the little copper wire egg-holders in the boxes of Easter-egg dye are about as useful for holding eggs as a *spork* is for eating in a fast food restaurant. Incidentally, I think the person who invented the spork should be tied to a chair at a table with a large tasty fried chicken breast on a plate in front of him and nothing but a spork and a plastic knife to eat it with. We'll see how soon he resorts to his fingers!

Anyway, I digress. As I said, egg dying and an egg hunt make a great combination. Like I mentioned before, schools are much less likely nowadays to allow their students to come over for a holiday visit. Nearby daycare centers will sometimes line up a trip or as I suggested previously, home-schooled social groups are another potential source of young people for intergenerational programming.

While the kids and residents are busy with their egg dying, you...*ahhhh*, I mean the *Easter Bunny*, can sneak away and hide candy and plastic eggs on the lawn - being sure to make several of them pretty tricky to find. Remember not to hide any near roads or driveways – and to relay that to the kids. You can buy plastic pre-filled eggs or schedule an egg-filling resident-volunteer group the day before the hunt. If the weather doesn't cooperate, you might be lucky enough to have an area inside the facility that will work. As the egg-coloring crew nears the end of their activity, the staff members, volunteers and the kids' parents should begin to bring residents to the egg-hunt site.

Once they have assembled, it's time to bring on the *hunters.* You will need to have a few sacks for any kids who didn't bring baskets. After a little plea to the older children to make sure the younger ones also find a few eggs, you can take a deep breath, rear back and let the whole thing rip. You will want to make sure that you and the parents have cameras primed and ready, since as you likely know, the kids can put locusts in a cornfield to shame. If only they would clean their rooms at home with that speed!

A ***tree-decorating party*** is a slightly sneaky way of providing the residents with a meaningful activity and simultaneously taking care of one of your holiday chores -

decorating the main Christmas tree. Rather than viewing tree decorating as another duty to fit in between your group activities, you can *turn it into one*. You will usually want to assemble the tree and string the lights the day before, but not turn them on yet. You'll likely need to set up a couple of long tables to hold the ornaments, which you can lay out in shallow boxes so they are easy to reach. Also, make sure you have enough ornament hangers.

If you don't have a huge resident population, you might be able to fit everyone in a semicircle (or possibly two) facing the tree. Then, to the accompaniment of Christmas music on a CD player, assist each resident in turn as they put two or three ornaments on the tree. In some cases you will need to help them fasten the ornaments firmly on the branches. Most likely, you will need to decorate the taller branches yourself but you can ask for direction from your residents as to exactly where to place each ornament. As staff members pass by, invite them in to hang an ornament. Once you've finished, it's time to turn out the room lights, count down from ten to one, then turn on the tree lights and sing "Oh Christmas Tree" (or at least the first two lines that most of us know). At the end of the group, you can check off "decorate the main Christmas tree" from your to-do list and will also have a tree that is truly the *residents'* Christmas tree.

In addition to these holiday festivities, there is a nearly endless string of **themed events** that can help us add some variety to the sameness of the resident's unchanging institutionalized schedule. Season-based occasions like Oktoberfest (yes, that's the way it's spelled), the Fourth of July, Mother's and Father's Day, St Patrick's Day, Mardi Gras and New Year's Eve celebrations help keep them in touch with the changing of the seasons.

Incidentally, a **New Year's Eve party in the afternoon** or early evening can have much the same feeling as the late-night version. Some lively entertainment, tasty snacks and a bit of the old "bubbly" can bring in the new year at 4:00 p.m. just as easily as at midnight. In fact, you can even rig up a New Year's Eve *ball-drop* with some bright-colored object hanging on a piece of string. If you run the string through a loop attached to the metal framework holding the ceiling tiles in place, you will be able to slowly lower your *Times Square* ball to the floor. Just raise the object to the ceiling (after a couple practice trials) and tie it off on a nearby chair or something...giving yourself plenty of slack and tying it with a slipknot.

Don't worry about trying to make it classy looking; the sillier it looks, the more fun it can be. We used a chili pepper piñata for our "New Year's Eve *pepper drop*." With a countdown, noisemakers, plastic glasses of champagne and a rousing chorus of Auld Lang Syne, you can bring in the new year with a bang. You might want to do your ball drop exactly on the hour - maybe four for an afternoon event or seven or eight for an evening party. Then, after looking it up the on the Internet, you can tell them they are helping the French (or whichever country's time zone correlates) celebrate their New Year's Eve.

And of course, some themed festivities can be programmed whenever you simply want to spice up the calendar. You can always pick a decade to celebrate with Roaring Twenties, Fabulous Fifties, Sizzling Seventies parties and the like. Events like Old West Days, Luau parties and Hooray for Hollywood socials can be scheduled whenever you want (although party stores traditionally stock Luau decorations for summer parties).

You can also pick an obscure anniversary to highlight, like Mickey Mouse's birthday or the invention of duct tape. On the more serious side, you could celebrate the anniversary of D-Day or the first moon landing. There are several great Internet resources that will help you keep track of these dates, like *HistoryOrb.com* and *On-This-Day.com*.

Exercise groups and modified sports add to the physical component of our activity programs. There are a number of exercising CD's and DVD's that are specially made for the folks we work with, like Sit and Be Fit, Chair Exercises for Seniors and the old standby, Sittercise. Adding "props" to the exercise moves can also make the experience a little more fun. Stretching lightweight elastic strips, waving colorful streamers and kicking beach balls back and forth can get folks exercising without even knowing they are doing it. Morning is traditionally a good time for a brief exercise program...often before a longer group activity. Usually ten or fifteen minutes will get the gang limbered up and ready to face the day.

Lightweight modified sporting equipment also adds color to our physical programming. Foam-rubber basketball tossing, Velcro darts, balloon volleyball, ring-toss, golf-putting, lightweight bowling, rubber horseshoes, bean-bag throws and the like can give the double benefit of providing the participants with a little workout and enjoyment at the same time. The equipment for all of these is available in our traditional supply catalogs as well as most large department stores. And we don't need to get tied up with game rules. Often we will simply gather the residents in a circle and move from one to the next, giving each participant several tries at tossing, putting or throwing. In fact, something as simple as lining residents up in two rows a few feet apart, and trying to keep a balloon in the air by tapping it back and forth can turn into a pretty lively affair.

And now, **a few words on bus rides and outings.** They, of course, can bring a welcome touch of the "outside world" to the residents. There are usually several routes you can take for a simple one-hour sightseeing bus ride. Simply driving around the neighborhood watching people walking their dogs or working in their yards can serve up a nice dose of normality. It is an added bonus if there is a specific site along the way, but a basic trip to a nearby small town to drive around Main Street and see the courthouse, schools and churches can work out just fine.

Similarly, we sometimes tend to feel that an outing needs to include a trip to the zoo, ball game or a museum. These can all be enjoyable (and sometimes pretty exhausting) but we should feel free to intersperse them with simpler less rigorous trips like a ride to a local ice cream shop or fast-food restaurant. In fact, I remember that at the end of a year in which we took our group to the Botanical Gardens, Atlanta's Coke Museum and the city zoo (with many *many* hills to climb), I asked which outings they had enjoyed the most. Two residents excitedly voiced their favorites. One chose a local hamburger joint and the other, a time-honored hotdog hangout we had visited. I believe that was the year I began to ratchet down the complexity of some of our outings.

There are a few tricks of the trade you will want to keep in mind. You should store small bottles of water as well as some energy bars in the bus, just in case you run into unexpected delays. Also on the safety side, make sure the bus has a first aid kit and fire extinguisher. If you are the *designated driver,* be sure you have a fully charged cell phone on hand (for emergency purposes only, of course). You will also need to be CPR certified. It would be great to always have a Certified Nursing Assistant with you on your rides and outings...but for budget and staffing reasons, that is often not the case.

For "get-off-the-bus" outings, however, you will definitely need another activity staff member or C.N.A. to accompany you. Volunteers, as you probably know, are also crucial to a successful outing. With a trip to a museum, botanical garden, historical site and other destinations that involve walking, one staff member or volunteer per resident is essential. Also - new activity directors, *listen up!* Even though a resident hikes freely around the facility on a cane or walker, you will want to pack a transport wheelchair for an outing that involves much walking. That individual is used to walking short distances in the facility, then sitting for a while. A walk around a museum or mall can be a *whole different story.*

So *newbies,* have I shot a good-sized dose of fear and anxiety into you with all this outing safety talk? Good, *keep it there.* Despite their obvious benefits, outings are basically chuck-full of "accidents waiting to happen." Make sure that behind your smiling relaxed expression, your eyes, ears and mind are fixed on your surroundings like

General Patten surveying a battlefield for land mines. And an outing's unexpected land mines can come in all forms - like volunteers who try to take too steep an incline with a resident in a wheelchair; an alert resident who wants to head off in another direction from the group or an unsteady resident who decides to stand up and head toward the restroom you just passed.

And of course, the toughest trial is yet to come. Yes, the most challenging part of the whole thing will usually occur after you have returned, unloaded everyone and are staggering toward your office with rivulets of perspiration streaming down your hair-matted forehead. That's when you may very likely encounter a staff member who smirks and remarks, "Well, it must be *nice* to just play and ride around all day." The challenge of course, lies in resisting the urge to yank the name tag off her uniform and stab her with the pin.

A ***Human Horse Race Game*** is one of those "just too cute" activities that never fails to brighten the day. I could have included it in the Racemania section, but I feel it deserves its own space. It is a natural for children, but I have seen adults get pretty excited as well. The race follows the same guidelines as Racemania but, as the name implies, the horses or other critters are replaced with people. You can either program a Human Horse Race as a full activity with several races, or as a one-time highlight to another event like a Grandparent's Day carnival or an associates' picnic.

First, you will need to lay out a track similar to the Racemania one, but you won't need rows - only five cross-lines. The racers will begin, lined up in numerical order, on one side of the first line and finish on the other side of the furthest line. In other words, they will step *across* the lines. This will give the winner five moves to the finish. You will want to use the blue painter's tape (so it can be easily removed without leaving a sticky residue).

Each racer can hold a large numbered card (one through six) or hang a pre-made sign around their neck. Just as with the other races, the "race fans" will name their human horse racers and select the number cards that match their favorite contestant. Other than requiring more space for the track, the game will proceed exactly like the smaller version. Keep this game in mind for Brownie and Daisy Scout visits, employee appreciations and holiday parties (reindeer antlers and rabbit ears add a festive touch) and be prepared for some *whooping and hollering*

"Bingo-banter" can add sparkle to our old friend, the traditional Bingo game. *Oh, stop rolling your eyes.* There's nothing wrong with Bingo; it's just that it sometimes tends to overshadow other activities that we have poured blood, sweat and tears into. I remember early on, when I had booked a county senior citizens' orchestra on what had traditionally been a Bingo afternoon. I helped the group carry in much of their equipment and many of their heavier instruments. After the concert, which incidentally was excellent, I again helped them tote their equipment back to their bus before I rearranged all the tables and chairs in the dining room where I had held it. As I was

adjusting the last chair and rubbing my aching muscles, a resident (who incidentally had thoroughly enjoyed the concert) raised a slightly disapproving eyebrow and inquired, "So...no Bingo today?" If I remember correctly, I didn't bother to inform her that I had rescheduled it for the following afternoon, and through slightly gritted teeth simply replied, "No."

It's not poor old Bingo's fault that it's so universally popular. But since it *is*, we might as well take advantage of that and add a little more sparkle to our overall program. A touch of showmanship and some slightly corny "bingo-banter" can help to add that sparkle. Rather than simply calling out the numbers, we can use number *nicknames*. G-55, for example, can become "double nickels" and I-16 could turn into "sweet sixteen." Any number in the I row could be an "eye ball" and B-12 could become the "vitamin pill." Little B-1 can become "baby bingo" and 0-75 can be the "granddaddy of Bingo."

Of course B-4 is a natural for "B-4...and after" and 0-66 can lead to "let's roll down Route 66 with 0-66." And if you are like many of us who have a few years under our belts, you might get a couple chuckles with, "And here's *my age*...I-21." Believe it or not, there are actually several websites listing potential Bingo number nick-names. Yes, of course, using them is silly - but not being afraid to show your silly side can make the residents feel that you are truly enjoying one of their favorite activities along with them.

The best present we can give them is to wash the thoughts of documentation deadlines, overdue bills and rising gas prices out of our heads for an hour. Then, as we breathe, smile, live in the present...and maybe even fire up our "silly side," we will give the impression that at that point in time, there is no where else we would rather be, and no other people we would rather be with. And sometimes as we reflect, relax and look around the room...that *might just be the case.*

Even though Bingo has gotten a bad rap from many activity professionals through the years, it is actually a pretty clever game with a neat history. Bingo has roots that reach back for centuries in France and Germany, but the version we know came from traveling carnivals and county fairs. A dealer would select numbered discs from a cigar box and the players would mark their cards with beans. It was called *Beano,* (decades before the anti-gas version came around).

In December of 1929, a New York toy merchandiser named Edwin Lowe ran across one of the games at a carnival near Jacksonville, Georgia. He arrived late in the evening and all of the carnival booths were closed except one - which was packed with people. As he stood on tiptoes to look over the shoulders of the onlookers, he saw the players excitedly putting beans on their cards when the pitchman called out a letter and number on their cards.

A 1930's
"Beano" game

When someone won, they shouted out, "Beano!" and would win a small Kewpie doll. Lowe tried to play the game that night and couldn't get a seat. "But while I was waiting around," he later recalled, "I noticed that the players were practically addicted to the game. The pitchman wanted to close up, but every time he said, 'This is the last game,' nobody moved. When he finally closed at 3:00 a.m. he had to chase them out."

Taking the idea back to New York, Lowe made a few adjustments, including a name change. According to reports, he invited friends and neighbors to his apartment to see how they liked the game. He soon found that they played with the same enthusiasm as the Georgia carnival-goers. Lowe said that at one of the games, a lady became more and more excited as each bean was added to her card. "Finally there was one number left," he remembered, "...and it was called! The woman jumped up, became tongue tied, and instead of shouting 'Beano,' stuttered 'B-B-B-Bingo'!" That catchy-sounding mistake would give a new name to a game that would be destined to entertain millions of people throughout the years...and net Mr. Lowe $26 million when he sold his game company to Milton Bradley in 1973.

During one recent game in our nursing center, the question somehow arose as to whether people play Bingo in heaven. One of our avid players snapped back, "Well of course they do. How else could it still be heaven?" To this day, I'm not quite sure if she was joking or dead serious.

Whether it's played in heaven or not, it darned sure better be on your activity schedule or you are a "dead activity director walking." When I was consulting back in the nineties, a fresh-off-the-vine therapeutic recreation specialist stated firmly that she planned on doing away with Bingo to show her residents how many other worthwhile activities she would be programming for them.

Although I did my best to dissuade her, I believe she actually did take it off the calendar. The next time I visited her, I noticed that twice-weekly Bingo games were printed prominently on the activity calendar. Although I wanted to ask, "So, how'd that 'taking Bingo off the calendar' thing work out for you, *huh?*" discretion ruled and neither of us ever mentioned it again.

And now...yes, still more Bingo tips. If you don't have the *Easy-read Finger-tip* large-print shutter cards, you might want to set a goal for buying them. They are not cheap by any means – at the time of this writing, about $68 for a 25-card set - but they work so much better than the cards that require chips. After years of pausing the game to help a nearsighted slightly confused lady who would lift up her card for a better view and scatter chips to the wind, we set our sights on obtaining the large-print shutter-cards. In fact, the proceeds of a couple of Raffle Auctions helped us seal the deal. Although the cards will eventually wear out, they are pretty sturdy.

And still another Bingo suggestion - after a lot of tinkering with other methods, I eventually settled on the system of never clearing the card throughout the entire game. If you clear the cards each time, you simply can't play many games. If you clear them after a specified number of games, you will usually need to roam around and make sure everyone has cleared their card.

Now, if you are a *fast-talking* Bingo caller, this won't work, but for me it did. As you might suspect from my *slight* tendency to ramble a bit and toss anecdotes into my writing, I'm not a direct *point A to point B* type of guy. Although you might get the occasional raised eyebrow, implying, "Are we here to talk or play Bingo?" most folks seem to enjoy a leisurely game. Taking your time and even tossing in an occasional joke or observation can let the residents know you are not rushing through one of their favorite activities to get to something else. You can also stretch out the suspense of the final coverall games with questions like "How many of you are down to just three numbers now?" Although, after asking how many were down to three, then later, "two," and then "one," I would usually query, "How many would like me to shut up and call Bingo?" This always produced a flurry of good-natured hand raising.

As a suggestion, if your budget can swing a ten-dollar game cost, you might give about seven or eight dollars in quarters during the straight and diagonal five-in-a-row games. This will leave two or three dollars for fifty-cent cover-all winners. That will let you play for three coveralls...which often turns into more on the last game. All in all, you will average about ten dollars a game. You can then come around with a prize cart filled with snacks of all varieties (remember to stock the sugar-free stuff) for those who want to trade in some or all of their quarters. Okay, I'm through with Bingo.

A *Who's Who Contest Display* involves pictures of residents and associates in their younger days. The best time-period for the photograph is likely from grade school through early marriage and family time. Most babies look pretty much alike and often pictures of adults are awfully easy to recognize. As with the other displays using photos, you will likely want to photocopy the pictures and give the original back to the participant. Also, this will give you the opportunity to reduce or enlarge the pictures as you copy them, so all the photos are about the same size.

Since the pictures are simply copies, you don't need to frame the display. Just cutting out the photocopied pictures and attaching them to several dark-colored poster boards with stick glue will work. You will want to place an easy-to-see number near each picture. Because the poster board display won't weight much, you can attach it to the wall with the 3M removable double-sided adhesive strips.

Of course, the idea of the contest display is to get people involved in guessing "who is who" and entering your contest. You will need to decide on an entry date when you want to receive the pictures and create a simple form containing the numbers for the photos entered and blank spaces beside them for the guesses. You will also want a contest ending date and time on the form. I would suggest delineating which photos are of residents and which are of staff members - maybe by adding an "R" or an "S" after the number on the label. Otherwise it is a little too difficult to determine who is who. As you can see from the example below, it gives kind of a nice *family-like* feeling to mix residents and associates on the same displays.

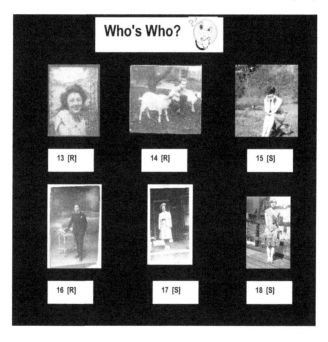

This contest always goes over well for National Nursing Home or Assisted Living celebrations. Since the purpose of the contest is purely for the enjoyment of guessing, the prize or prizes for the most correct guesses won't need to be extravagant. Usually large bags of Cracker Jacks or animal crackers will suffice. Besides, in most cases, staff members will team up anyway, trading names of people they have recognized, in exchange for those they are having trouble with. Don't feel like you need to "patrol" this kind of collusion. It brings people together and besides, it's only for Cracker Jacks anyway.

A current events group can help keep residents up to date on events around them. One group that combines several aspects is **In The News**. It seems to include a good mixture of intellectual stimulation and fun. During the group, you can read interesting articles from the national and local sections of the day's newspaper. You will want to allow a few minutes prior to the group to select the articles you are going to read, so it doesn't look as if you simply sat down with the newspaper and selected them as you went along. In some cases, you will likely read only the first several paragraphs. Another staple of a good current events group can be a brief overview of the daily horoscope, ending with the words of wisdom from either Dear Abby or Ann Landers, depending upon which day you schedule the group.

You might also be familiar with a useful product called *News Currents*. It consists of a DVD program of still pictures of people and events that made the news the previous week - along with a corresponding script that provides information and suggestions for discussion topics. The great thing about the program is that it provides visuals along with the current events information. The down side is (at the time of printing) it costs nearly eight dollars per week for the weekly DVD and newssheet. Of course this includes the shipping and they do send it out quickly...usually arriving by midweek the next week. There is also an on-line version.

Incidentally, you are not destroying the first amendment if you don't read some topics or sections of articles you feel might be too gory or depressing for your folks. People can always listen to the television news to hear more on those. We don't need to *sugar coat* the news, but there's really nothing to be gained by covering a horrific accident that might leave everyone depressed. By the same token, however, although we may want to skip over a word or two in Dear Abby or Ann Landers from time to time, the *hot-button* topics often covered in those columns, can produce some pretty spirited conversations.

Navigating Around
The Barriers

Most of the activities we have been discussing have been *open-attendance* groups for individuals who function on a high or moderately high cognitive level. Unfortunately, of course, many of the residents we work with are not able to get much benefit out of them. For these individuals, we are going to need to ratchet down both our expectations and the complexity of the activities themselves.

The barriers we encounter too often handicap us in our attempts to reach the part of the individual that is still working and unbroken. When I think of handicaps, though, I remember a blind artist I met years ago at a mall in Florida. She was displaying a number of beautiful paintings she had recently completed. A sign in the display area explained that she was totally blind.

I bought one of her smaller works and asked what technique she used. In a very upbeat manner, she told me how she would envision a scene in her mind and stick plastic-headed pins in the canvas where she visualized the main focal points of the work. If it was a landscape, she said the pins would mark various trees, rocks, animals and so forth. For a floral still life, she might stake out the pins to represent the centers of the flowers, the ends of leaves or the outside dimension of a vase.

The next step, she explained, was to wrap string around the heads of the pins about an inch above the canvas. This system gave her a network of strings to guide her fingers along the major points of the planned piece of art. She would then squeeze paint onto her palette; always keeping the palette's colors in the same order. Then she would apply the paint by following along the string above the canvas and touching down with a small piece of sponge she had dipped in the paint. She said it was definitely a times-taking process and that she couldn't take a break from the picture or she would lose her concentration.

As she was finishing her explanation, a lady walked up and told her that she had painted some beautiful pieces despite her handicap. The artist thanked her, but said she really thought of her blindness as more of a "hassle" than a handicap. She said she viewed it as a hassle to be overcome in doing what she wanted to do in her life.

That common-sense approach helped her overcome one hassle after the next until she reached her goal of becoming a professional painter. Incidentally, she said she had never painted before she lost her sight, but had simply heard of this technique from another blind painter and followed suit. That concept, of viewing what most people think of in terms of handicaps that block the way - as hassles to be overcome, seems like a positive and practical way to approach residents with cognitive problems.

We will definitely encounter *hassles* along the path as we strive to reach the well and healthy sections of the brain that the enemies of the mind have not destroyed. Those ruthless enemies, like stroke, Alzheimer's Disease and all their treacherous comrades, ruthlessly bombard the inner walls of the poor victim's brain. Fortunately, in the midst of the destruction, small *pockets of resistance* often hide behind those battered walls. Those pockets harbor long-term memories that are not only still alive, but can be triggered to revive some of the feelings of enjoyment and serenity that once inhabited the individual's peaceful mental landscape.

Often the enemy has ravaged the parts of the brain that transform symbols into mental objects that the individual can visualize in his or her mind. Words, in fact, are simply a meaningless string of symbols unless we are able to convert them into what they stand for. Luckily, the ability to recognize objects often hides out in some of the brain's safe havens and avoids the ravages of battle. So, even though the phrase, "Do you remember your first sewing machine?" might produce a blank look - a picture or illustration of an old Singer sewing machine could elicit a smile of remembrance because it is an **object** still contained in the **long-term memory**. This realization can help us navigate around many hassles in programming for cognitively impaired residents.

So as we work around the hassles of short-term memory loss and the lack of symbol recognition, we still have a pretty good arsenal of activities at our disposal. In a higher-level group like the Hometown Discussion, we could start an interaction among the participants with a question like "What was your first automobile?" But with the folks we're discussing now, we will include an object-recognition approach like showing the residents a picture or illustration of a Model T Ford. Even with those who still have some ability to understand questions, the picture will help reach those memories quicker than merely talking.

As you likely know, we will need to modify our group activities in a couple other ways as well. Since we will need to spend more time with each resident, the group size will often shrink to three or four participants. We are also going to be looking for a fairly quiet, low-stimulus area because of limited attention spans. Fortunately there are several interesting groups that fill the bill for these requirements. Here are a few that have proven successful:

A **modified reminiscence group** might be called something like Back in the Day or The Good Old Days. Keeping in mind the need for stimulating the object-recognition ability, we will use sturdy antiques and reminiscing pictures. Several varieties of reminiscing picture cards are available from our usual suppliers, including: Everyday Life Photos (*Children & family Life* and *A Grown-up's World* sets); the Americana Nostalgic Postcard Series and the Bi-Folkal nostalgic photo collection:

As with most modified small groups, the length of the activity itself will need to shrink. Usually twenty or twenty-five minutes will do. The activity might consist of only three residents and the group leader sitting around a small table. As the leader shows pictures and antiques to the residents, he or she will try to encourage some type of interaction among the participants. The pictures cards are designed to elicit recollections of early automobiles, school classes, weddings, children's games, holiday celebrations and other universal memories.

For obvious reasons, we won't be using breakable antiques, but a number of items from earlier days, hold up well. Objects like old Prince Albert pipe tobacco tins, kitchen tools, metal medicine tins, children's blocks and tin toys like these can take some pretty good abuse:

As we use the photo cards and objects, we need to keep in mind that our goal, unlike that of a speech therapist who uses similar tools, is not to "test" the participants' memories, but to encourage an enjoyable interaction. Even if someone is using the wrong words, the smile of remembrance as he or she looks at the picture of a young mother giving her baby a bath, tells us that our activity is working. The goal we are striving for is simply to emulate the enjoyable memory-evoking *chats* that the residents once had around the kitchen table or out on the front porch.

Name That Tune

Memories of songs often last long after other memories and abilities have disappeared. Most of us have been amazed when a resident who usually doesn't communicate, starts softly mouthing the words to Amazing Grace during a church service. A **modified version of Name That Tune** can take advantage of that situation.

This group seems to be successful in a larger setting than some of the other low-level activities. The Sound Choice reminiscing CD's I mentioned on page 89, work well for Name That Tune. Starting with the non-vocal version of a familiar song, you might play it for about 30-seconds, then ask if anyone recognizes the song. Unlike the crossword puzzle I discussed previously, you are going to need to give some easy hints.

If nobody guesses the song, The Yellow Rose of Texas, for example, you might say, "I think it's about a flower...maybe a yellow rose of...." If someone says, "Texas," you can respond with a hearty "good job." If not, we're still not through. You might say, "I'll bet it's about a state, like Texas or Oklahoma. Which one do you think it might be?" Even if someone selects Oklahoma, you can say, "No, and that leaves Texas. I think we've got it!" In other words, as with the reminiscence pictures, we want to make sure that nobody feels like they are being tested and failed.

After the song is identified, you can play the vocal version, and the group members can listen or sing along. Once the song is through, it's time to select another non-vocal track to play for about 30-seconds and start the guessing process again. About seven or eight songs makes a good length for the activity. A volunteer who enjoys music and feels comfortable working with cognitively impaired residents might take on this group. Incidentally, a higher-level version of Name That Tune using the same concept, minus the obvious clues, makes a good 25 to 30-minute group to combine with another short activity.

We can't forget good old Bingo with these folks too. Keeping the need for object-recognition in mind, **simplified versions of Bingo** can be successful, like the color and shape-matching games below. School supply catalogs and stores carry several varieties:

From experience, you will want to use large pasteboard or cardboard markers, rather than red poker chips. To a confused individual, the chips can look like candy wafers. You will likely need to give quite a bit of assistance to some players. As with the reminiscing group, three players seated around a table is plenty and allows the group leader the opportunity to help each player in turn.

With a modified bingo game, you can provide a bit of the same suspense in the higher-level version. Most of these modified games use only eight or nine spaces and either three or four matches in a row will win the game. As a resident nears the end, you might pump a little enthusiasm into the game with comments like, "George has two already. If he gets a green square, he'll win." As you might suspect, the game continues until all three participants have won. Snack cakes, crackers and such work well for the winners' prizes.

Now, let's combine the reminiscing group with the modified bingo game, for a game I call **"Remember When" Bingo**. This is one I dreamed up recently that uses object recognition to connect with long-term memories, in a fun game setting. The card below contains photographs of nine memory-eliciting antiques.

Incidentally, the item on the top right of the card is a "darning egg" used to insert into a sock to hold it in place while you stitched up a hole. And yes, ladies dyed their stockings with the Tintex stocking dye. Sometimes it's amazing the memories items like these will trigger...and the things you can learn, even from residents functioning on a relatively low cognitive level.

Since this is intended for a small group, you will only need to create four cards. Each card can be made using printable card stock. The nine squares are easily formed with the "table" function of Microsoft Word by setting the table size for three columns and three rows. Once you create the table, you will be able to stretch the size of each section by hitting the space bar under each of the three horizontal lines. You can then left-click the curser on the two inner vertical lines and drag them to even the size of the blocks. You will want to create four page-sized cards like the one on the previous page, using the *copy and paste* function. At this point, you will not have any pictures in the blanks.

If this isn't your cup of tea, ask a Geek friend to help. Keep in mind, of course, that if you don't want to create a computer-made version, you can always resort to scissors, stick glue and real live pictures. But even though I am no spring chicken and did cut-and-paste projects by actually "cutting" and "pasting," I would suggest using the computer or conning a family member or volunteer into making you a set. It just looks classier.

You can obtain the pictures by utilizing the "images" function of a search engine like Google. I would suggest first creating a folder named Remember When Bingo, in *my documents* or *my pictures*. As you call up a cool looking antique, click on the image, which will connect you to the website. Then, put your cursor over the picture, right-click and hit "save picture as...."

Incidentally, I wouldn't get all tied up in copyright concerns regarding the photographs. Most of the antiques you'll find are simply pictures of items people are trying to sell. Even if they are from an educational or other professional website, we are not making money with the reproductions and are simply using them to brighten the days of senior citizens.

Once you see the Save Picture screen, click on the folder you have prepared and save the selected picture, using whatever file name you prefer. You can simply use "1," "2," "3" etc. if you want. You will need to do this with 18 pictures. Then you will need to *format* the pictures (look back to the top of page 66) so they won't jump around and make you crazy when you work with them.

Now, take heart, this is really not as time consuming as it might sound. You will shrink the pictures to fit inside the blocks by pulling in the corner of the picture with your curser. Then copy and paste one of the antique pictures in a block on two different cards (not in the same place on each one). Now, go back to your *Remember When Bingo* folder in My Pictures, copy another picture and also paste it into random blanks on two of the cards. Continue to do this with all eighteen pictures until your four cards are filled. Since you will usually play with either three or four players, this will provide you with at least one match each time, but not more than two.

Now, you have two possibilities for selecting the antique items on the cards. If you plan to collect some of the things I mentioned previously in the section about the modified reminiscence group, they will become your Bingo "calling objects." Just put the eighteen small items in a bucket and select them one at a time. If someone has a match, they can cover the picture. For flat items, you can scan them and save the picture as we discussed. If they cannot easily be scanned, you can usually find a very similar antique using the Google image function.

If you are not going to use actual objects, you will need to print out larger versions of the images to use for calling. You will likely want to have the set laminated for protection. School and office supply stores will usually be able to laminate four cards on a large sheet...usually for a couple bucks each sheet. Then just cut them apart. Be sure to turn in an invoice to the business office for your printer ink and lamination cost.

Of course, as you show the antique or picture calling card, you will have the opportunity to promote memory sharing among the participants. Incidentally, if you're not into creating a set yourself, just email me at the address on the title page, and I'll be glad to email back complimentary pictures of the one I made. You can simply print them onto heavy-weight copy paper, cut out the playing and calling cards and laminate the set.

In the physical-activity category, the **lightweight sports equipment** I mentioned earlier, will come in handy. A foam-rubber basketball toss, beach ball kick or ring-toss can be programmed in a large circle, moving from resident to resident. Needless to say, there are no game rules involved. Get ready, of course, to do a little crawling around retrieving balls and rings. Incidentally, modified sports make *wonderful* activities to organize when you have teenage volunteers around.

Puzzle-time involves large-piece jigsaw puzzles. A number of our suppliers carry simplified jig saw puzzles ranging from 4-piece to 28-piece puzzles. They come with a picture of the completed puzzle that can be laid out next to the puzzle pieces. This activity seems to work best when pairs of residents are teamed up at several tables. The group leader can spend a few minutes at each table assisting the puzzlers as needed. As with all of the activities in this section, the primary focus is not on the skills required, but the socializing and enjoyment of the activity. As you can see from the examples below, there are some pretty captivating pictures available.

Working with individuals who are extremely restricted in their abilities and awareness can, as we all know, become pretty discouraging. But as disappointing as fighting the hassles and obstacles can be, especially for the minimal response we trigger, it is definitely worth the effort. We will never, of course, bring them back to the times when they played catch with their children, attended neighborhood card parties and had "dinner on the ground" with their family at church functions. But our efforts might still reach a few of those pockets of resistance that harbor the remnants of their once-vital personalities back when *they* were *us*. Sometimes, as my poem on the next page attests, we need to look very deeply to see the person behind the barriers.

Looking Deeply

by Dennis Goodwin

Looking at her, from the doorway
I first felt the stillness.
Sitting in the half-lit room,
her face wearing the lines of time,
she stared out through smudged glasses
seemingly into nothing at all;
rocking slowly, humming tunelessly.

Ready to turn and walk away,
the soft and steady humming
drew me slowly closer.
As I leaned closer still,
the sounds, so far away at first,
took on the words of children's songs.
Chanting and laughing,
they slowly brought light into the room.

"Mommy," they called out,
"You said it's time for pie."
And as quickly as the sounds had changed,
the smell - the musty smell of age
disappeared; replaced with
apples and cinnamon and
the thousand smells of springtime.

Her eyes, so dull at first,
now danced across her face.
"All right, you little beggars,"
she laughed into the sunshine,
"Come in and sit yourselves."
And as the skipping ropes hit the ground,

the children gathered; singing and laughing
and taking turns on mommy's lap.
But the sounds of licking spoons
and tender giggles
began to fade away.
And just as suddenly as before,
the laughing sounds became again
the nameless tune.
The sun-lit yard dimmed
and faded into time.
Slowly, the lines reappeared
on her time-worn face.

But still staring out through smudged glasses,
her eyes had somehow changed.
Looking deeply now, I saw reflected,
the faces of laughing children
and the serenity of springtime.

In the forty-some-some years since I entered the long-term care activity field, quite a bit has changed. One thing that remains constant, however, is that it is still populated with caring talented individuals. Like everyone else, they have car problems, money troubles, sinus headaches and all the rest. But unlike their co-workers, who feel free to occasionally gripe and grumble. they are pretty much expected to wear their happy perky faces throughout the day. Hopefully the Best-dressed Pet Show, Root Beer & Roulette, Human Horseracing and the rest can add a little genuine *perk* to the hard-working soft-hearted activity professionals behind those permanently perky faces.

I hope you have enjoyed our little visit. I definitely did. I also included several of my ten-minute read-aloud short stories. I am a bit of a history buff and have been writing real-life short stories since dinosaurs roamed the earth. These and many more are in my "History Makers" series, available through ElderSong and other resources, and include thought provoking discussion-starter questions.

Activity directors have found them useful in both individual and group programming. They work well as a part of one of the "cluster" activities I mentioned on page four. The stories are brief and fit limited attention spans.

Thanks for taking the time to read my book, and happy programming!

Making Mayberry

The creation of "America's town"

The small rock was perfect – nice and round, just right for a good ripple-making plunk. And the little fellow who pitched it toward the lake just couldn't be any more wholesome and all-American. He had the ideal country-boy mop of tousled hair to match his innocent freckled faced smile. When the CBS television cameras focused on the view in the summer of 1960, it seemed like the ideal background for the opening credits of their new show. And it certainly was, except for one problem. The rock fell short of the water and bounced along the ground. The same thing happened with the second take. Their little six-year-old rock-pitcher, Ronnie Howard, just didn't have the strength to toss it from their path all the way to the lake.

The scene, however, was too idyllic to scrap. The show's assistant director, Bruce Bilson, soon conceived another strategy. He hid a prop man behind a bush on the set. This time, when Ronnie tossed the rock, Bilson yelled "Throw it!" Deceiving all but the most perceptive viewers, who may have noticed a little longer-than-normal lag time before the rock touched down, the switch worked perfectly. Cut! Print! Team it up with a bouncy tune and some perky whistling, and you've ready to kick off a long string of colorful homespun stories. Those stories, and the cast of characters who enacted them, would one day turn the fictitious little town they inhabited into a lasting symbol of wholesome country values – *Mayberry*.

Like the rock-throwing opening, the series that created Mayberry, first needed a little tinkering. Emerging during an episode of *The Danny Thomas Show*, the skit that would develop into The *Andy Griffith Show* featured Andy as a country bumpkin sheriff who arrested Thomas for running a stop sign. Also in the skit were Ronnie Howard as Andy's son, and Frances Bavier as a back-country lady named Henrietta Perkins. She would eventually play Aunt Bee on the resulting series.

Andy's character was themed after his popular comedy monologues like "What it was, was football." Unlike his later contemplative country-philosopher style, he was a cast as a heavy-handed hillbilly sporting a devious ear-to-ear grin.

Despite the need for a few tweaks, the episode stirred up positive reviews and put plans in motion for a new show. The producers decided it would be set in the present time but reflect the values of an earlier, more relaxed era. "Though we never said it, and though it was shot in the '60s," Andy Griffith later philosophized, "it had a feeling of the '30s." That drift back into an earlier, simpler time, would fulfill a desire for millions of viewers to briefly escape from the real-life social turmoil of the decade. As visions of a war-torn Vietnam and police dogs attacking civil rights protestors flashed across their television screens, the timeless rustic inhabitants of Mayberry helped calm their jangled nerves.

Andy, prior to his successful mid-fifties comedy monologues, had dreamed of quite a different career destination than Mayberry. His first ambition was to become an opera singer. Somewhere along the line, his vision shifted to that of a music teacher. Perhaps the mental image of his standing on the opera stage, likely in tights, didn't look any better to him than to most of us. After teaching music in a high school for three years, he and his wife, Barbara, set off for careers in entertainment. Together, they developed a traveling routine that featured their singing and dancing as well as Andy's comedy monologues. Soon, Andy would flourish both on Broadway and in the movies. He successfully performed the role of Will Stockdale in the 1955 play, *No Time for Sergeants* and in the later movie version.

His co-star in both the play and movie was Morgantown, West Virginia actor, Don Knotts. He had perfected the ability to portray a hilarious little bug-eyed fidgety character. In real life, he was actually quite relaxed and laid back. The two formed a close friendship that lasted for the rest of their lives. As with Griffith and his popular comedy routines, Knotts had also managed to remain in the public eye, portraying a variety of zany characters in Steve Allen's "Man on the Street" interviews. When Knotts heard his buddy would be playing a small-town sheriff in his upcoming show, he didn't hesitate to call him. "You got a deputy?" he quizzed. Andy instantly realized the value in their teaming up again.

One by one, Andy and the production staff began to populate their little town with residents. Andy, they decided, would be a widower, but should have family...maybe a young son. Their choice, six-year-old Ron Howard, then known as "Ronnie," had already racked up some showbiz credits. Coached by his father, Vance, an accomplished character actor, Ronnie had made appearances in television shows like Johnny Ringo, the Twilight Zone, and Dennis the Menace. Both Andy and Ron would later say that their on-screen reactions with each other stemmed from their warm relationships with their own fathers. Andy's proud nod, for example, when little Opie hit the lake with his rock (even though we now know he didn't) came from his father's customary nod of approval.

Frances Bavier, like most of the other Mayberry characters, was no stranger to acting. With professional acting roots tracing back to the 1930's, she was a former cast member of *The Eve Arden Show* and had her own mid-fifties sitcom, *It's a Great Life*. Similarly, Howard McNear, who played the scatter-brained but lovable barber, Floyd Lawson, had cut his teeth in various television roles. He had also played Doc Adams on the radio version of *Gunsmoke*. Although most of the emerging cast had similar backgrounds, one was a total greenhorn to television. Griffith discovered Jim Nabors singing in a Southern California night club. Originally written in for only a single episode, Nabors' "Gomer Pyle" soon became an integral citizen of Mayberry.

The first episode aired on October 3rd, 1960 to lukewarm reviews, but excellent ratings. Early in the first season, Andy's character, like both his roles on the Danny Thomas episode and in *No Time for Sergeants*, strove for the majority of the laughs.

After reviewing the second episode, however, a light flashed on in Griffith's mind. *My God*, he thought, *I just realized that I'm the straight man.* The outlandish antics of Barney, Floyd, Gomer, Opie, Ernest T. Bass, Aunt Bee, and the others stirred up plenty of laughs – he didn't really need to join them. "I'm playing straight to all these kooks around me," he decided. In an interview years later, he reflected on his transformation from the funny guy to the straight man. "I never regretted it," he confirmed, "the straight man has the best part. He gets to be in the show and see it too."

Andy wasn't the only one who wanted to see the show. It never left the Top Ten throughout its eight-year run. Even with Knotts leaving after five years and Andy after six, the magic of Mayberry continued. Although each of its eventual 249 episodes has its followers, in polls of fan club members, they often chose "Man in a Hurry" as the one that personifies the show. Aired in January of 1963, the show involved an impatient businessman from Charlotte whose car broke down in Mayberry on a Sunday. Originally complaining about the sluggish ways of Gomer and the other Mayberry inhabitants, he encountered Andy, Aunt Bee, Opie, and the rest. By the end of the episode, they had worked their small-town charms on him and he decided to stay around for a while even after his car was fixed. Like millions of fans, he realized there was something very special about Mayberry – *America's town.*

"In Madness or Melancholy"

The deceitful obituary intended to destroy
Edgar Allan Poe's legacy, which actually enhanced it

"Edgar Allan Poe is dead," the obituary flatly stated. "He was at all times a dreamer, dwelling in ideal realms – in heaven or hell – peopled with creatures and the accidents of his brain." The obituary went on to inform readers that not only were Poe's visions *peopled with creatures*, but the poet and short-story writer was, himself, quite an odd creature: "He walked the streets in madness or melancholy, with lips moving in indistinct curses, or with eyes upturned in passionate prayers."

The obituary was first printed in the *New York Tribune* on October 9, 1849, and later reprinted around the world. Its author, Rufus W. Griswold, using the pseudonym Ludwig for anonymity, painted a vivid word-picture of his former friend, Edgar Allan Poe. He portrayed him as having been as tormented as his bizarre tails and as morose as his heart-rending poems. It was a history-making appraisal that would mold the public's opinion of Poe for the next century. It was also something else – a fictitious load of nonsense.

Griswold, a literary rival of Poe, had once been the target of one of Edgar's cutting critiques in a literary magazine. The cut never healed, leaving Griswold looking for revenge. Despite his attempt to destroy Poe's reputation, Griswold later decided to make money off his name. He convinced Edgar's mother to sign away the rights of his works, and he published a collection of Poe's stories and poetry. At the time of Edgar's untimely demise at the age of forty, however, Griswold had only one goal – to publish a scandalous slur that would forever bury his rival's legacy.

Much like one of Edgar Allan Poe's immortal short stories, Griswold's delight in his *burial* of Poe's legacy, was a bit "premature." Advancing the concept of Poe as a madman writing about other madmen, simply aroused the public's

147

curiosity and increased the sales of his writing. Despite another attempt by Griswold to smear his nemesis in a larger, but equally libelous biography, his plans failed dismally. As the decades passed, Poe's influence on literature skyrocketed. Eventually, legitimate biographers replaced the vision of Poe as a raving madman, with that of a troubled but brilliant author and poet. Rufus Griswold, on the other hand, is usually thought of – if at all – simply as Edgar Allan Poe's first biographer.

Although Poe didn't walk the streets in madness or melancholy, he was likely never accused of being particularly mentally healthy either. His youth was plagued with loss, which probably seeded the clouds of darkness that would hover over much of his life. Born in Boston to actor parents, Edgar's father, David Poe, abandoned the family, and his mother, Elizabeth, died before Edgar's third birthday. He and his brother and sister were scattered to different foster homes. He wound up in the family of a wealthy exporter in Richmond, Virginia named John Allan. The family's last name served as his middle name, since as far as literary historians know, he previously didn't have one.

The dark subjects and settings that would flow through his writings would lead most to expect young Edgar to have been an angst-filled loner as a teenager. Like his genre-bending work, though, his life was difficult to categorize under what *might be expected.* The young Poe was actually quite athletic – competing in foot races, boxing, and the running broad jump. He became locally famous by swimming six miles upstream in Virginia's James River. In addition, although we might expect him to introduce himself in a haunting, muffled voice as *Edgar Allan Poe*, he preferred the name "Eddy."

Young *Athletic Eddy*, seemed to be the ideal candidate to follow his foster father into his business ventures. The business forms Edgar's father set in front of his son, however, often wound up with scribbled lines of poetry on the back. Edgar just couldn't contain his love for the rhymes, rhythm, and emotional fervor of popular poets like his new-found hero, Lord

Byron. As might be expected, their relationship left something to be desired – and, in fact, left nothing in his rich father's will for the striving young poet. But like his father, Edgar developed a strong determination to succeed in business. His business success, though, would not be created with rows of numbers, but with lines of words.

It would be years before those lines would sustain him. At 18, he lied about his age and served a two-year stretch in the Army, eventually even entering the U. S. Military Academy at West Point. Before long, he decided he was not officer material and stopped attending classes or formations in order to receive a dismissal. Although he didn't sparkle in military matters, he did kick off his writing career during this time. He self-published 50 copies of a small book of poetry titled *Tamerlane and Other Poems*. Not expecting it to carve his name into the annals of literature, he simply signed it, "by a Bostonian."

Unfortunately, his expectations were correct and the little book received no attention. This was also the case with his second venture two years later in 1829, when he published a little larger book, titled *Al Araaf, Tamerlane and Minor Poems*. Summoning his determination for success, he tried a third book in February of 1831. During his time at West Point, he had garnered a few readers among the other cadets, with satirical verses about their commanding officers. Several of them coughed up 75 cents each to help pay the publishing fee. Poe again included his previous poems, but added several new ones, including "To Helen and "The City in the Sea."

This one garnered a little more attention, as did his articles and critiques in literary journals throughout the years ahead. His short stories also began to attract a number of readers, especially a mystery tale about a new species of bug, which resembled a skull. As the story proceeds, the unusual "gold bug" inadvertently leads the narrator and his friend toward untold riches. The little page-turner suddenly lit a flickering spotlight on a new American writer – Edgar Allan Poe.

That spotlight, though, would not fully illuminate him until January of 1845. Inspired by a talking bird in Dickens' novel, *Barnaby Rudge*, Poe wrote a dark but beautiful allusion-packed poem delving into loss, fear, and madness. He later wrote that, in his mind there "arose the idea of a non-reasoning creature, capable of speech." His first thought, he noted, was to use a parrot, but this idea was "superseded forthwith by a Raven, as equally capable of speech." That second thought would give birth to one of his most famous works. Good thing, since "quoth the parrot," wouldn't have packed quite the same lyrical impact.

Before Poe would leave us, he populated the literary world with an intense array of characters who would keep his legend very much alive. The analytical genius, C. Auguste Dupin, who solved the mystery of the double murder in Rue Morgue and discovered the whereabouts of a vitally important purloined letter, would influence countless mystery writers to come. Sir Arthur Conan Doyle, the creator of Sherlock Holmes, confirmed Poe's standing, once asking, "Where was the detective story until Poe breathed the breath of life into it."

Poe also took us into a dark world where wildly beating hearts tell tales of grisly murders, virulent plagues hide behind party masks, and black cats reveal incriminating evidence. No, Edgar Allan Poe may not have walked the streets in madness, but he might have cracked the door open a few times to take a peek at it. In his own words, perhaps not meant entirely tongue-in-cheek, he once explained, "I became insane, with long intervals of horrible sanity."

Hilarious Hillbillies

The birth of television's *Beverly Hillbillies*

"We drove to Abraham Lincoln's cabin and visited the battlefields of historic places," television writer, Paul Henning, reflected. As was often the case, during this trip in the late 1950s, his fertile imagination busily concocted colorful scenarios to help relieve the boredom of the open road. Sharing his vision, he told his family, "Imagine someone from that Civil War era sitting here in this car with us, going sixty miles an hour down a modern highway." As he considered it, he realized the humor that could arise from the misunderstandings the time-traveler might have about contemporary society. That daydream was the germ of a television program that would make most critics turn up their noses. But the show, *The Beverly Hillbillies*, would also put smiles on the faces of over fifty-five million viewers every week.

He soon realized the concept wouldn't require introducing someone from the past, but simply somebody who wasn't familiar with modern conveniences. Henning's thoughts traveled back to his days as a Boy Scout in his home state of Missouri. He had attended a scout camp near the Arkansas border. The leaders would take the scouts on long hikes into the woods where they would often run across folks who lived a very basic life. "I found there were pockets of people who resisted modernization," he recalled. All he would need to do, Henning mused, was to transport some of them to a bustling city, to have the same effect as bringing in people from the past. First, he considered New York City but decided it would cost too much to film there. Besides, he and his family were firmly rooted in Los Angeles and didn't want to move. *Beverly Hills,* he decided, would be perfect.

During the months ahead, his hazy daydream began to crystallize into a concrete program idea. Soon, he would have the opportunity to pitch it to some CBS television executives.

Through the years, Henning had worked his way up the entertainment ladder, first in radio script-writing, then television. He and his future wife, Ruth Barth, had teamed up at Kansas City's KMBC radio – co-writing and acting out country-themed serials like *Happy Hollow* and *Life on the Red Horse Ranch*. In 1928, the station became part of the Columbia Broadcasting System. Separately, both Paul and Ruth transferred to CBS in Chicago to work for several radio shows, including *Fibber McGee and Molly*. By the next year, their partnership had turned romantic. They married and moved to the studio's Los Angeles headquarters.

During the next twenty years, Paul became firmly entrenched in the California radio and television field, while Ruth turned her attention toward their growing family. He wrote for Eddie Cantor, Rudy Vallee, and George Burns & Gracie Allen. His successful reputation as a writer slowly elevated him to the status of a respected voice in the company. As a result, during a meeting in 1959, a programming executive asked him if he had any ideas for a future television show. In response, Paul crossed his fingers and pitched his recent vision of backwoods characters transplanted into a modern city. After he had finished, he looked tentatively around the table, fearing he would see perplexed gazes. Instead, he was greeted with nodding heads and growing smiles. Over the next couple years, those nods and smiles transformed into financial and production support for his pet project.

As Henning's imagination shifted into high gear, the program's characters began to materialize. They could be a family from the secluded hill country of the Ozarks, like those he had met on his scout hikes. From the start, he knew exactly who he wanted to portray Jed Clampett, the head of the household – Buddy Ebsen. Henning had been watching him play the sidekick, George Russell, on Disney's *Davy Crockett*, and felt he made the "perfect hillbilly." Ebsen's acting career reached back years before this *hillbilly* period, to his song-and-dance premier in *Broadway Melody of 1936*. Three years later, he was selected to play the Scarecrow in *The Wizard of Oz.* Ray Bolger, originally cast as the Tin Man, decided he wanted to switch to the Scarecrow. Ebsen didn't have a problem with that and traded with him. Unfortunately, after several days in rehearsal, he developed a severe allergic reaction to the metallic dust in the Tin Man makeup, and had to be replaced. Over twenty years later, though, his standout role as Jed Clampett more than made up for his loss.

Henning briefly considered creating the role of a mother for Jed, in the character of Daisy May Clampett or "Granny." Then he realized she would be the matriarch of the family, and he wanted Jed to be the head of the clan. No problem, he thought, Granny can be Jed's mother-in-law. His first choice for the role was actually veteran actress, Bea Benaderet. He was a little concerned however, that she didn't fit the physical look he had in mind for Granny, since Bea was a little "busty." Bea agreed and suggested her friend Irene Ryan for the role. Like Benederet, Ryan had made her mark in radio and television through the years. An observer of Ryan's tryout said that when she read for the role "with her hair tied back in a bun, and feisty as all get-out," both the executive producer, Al Simon, and Henning blurted out, "That's granny!" Benaderet was later assigned the role of Jed's cousin, Pearl Bodine, and eventually starred as Kate Bradley on *Petticoat Junction.*

Jed's only child, Elly May, wasn't feisty like Granny, but despite her pinup girl appearance, was quite the tomboy. In fact, she could "rassle" just about any fellow to the ground. Despite this, she had a soft heart, especially when it came to the "critters" she gathered around her like fuzzy family members. Selected from among 500 others, Louisiana-born actress, Donna Douglas, fit Elly May's role perfectly. Reflecting on her audition, she remembered they tied up a goat on the set and asked her if she could milk it. "Well, I had never milked a goat in my life," she later confided, "but I said, 'sure, I can milk that goat.' " This bold answer, even if untrue, snagged her the role. "Over the nine years, I probably worked with over 900 animals," she recalled. "Elly didn't kiss a lot of men, but she sure kissed a lot of critters." The critters weren't the only ones to admire the blue-jean-clad beauty. "Donna Douglas has done more for the sale of blue jeans," a Levi executive once declared, "than cowboys have done in a hundred."

And of course the family would not have been complete without Jethro Bodine, the son of Jed's cousin, Pearl. Actor, Max Baer Jr, was an ideal choice for the role. Though Jethro wasn't rocket-scientist material, his family proudly boasted of his "sixth-grade education." This *higher education,* Jethro figured, should net him a good job. In various episodes, he tried to parley it into the pre-requisite for an Air Force general, psychiatrist, and brain surgeon. In most cases, however, his interest in these elusive professions stemmed from pretty girls he might impress with the titles. He not only loved girls, he loved all things edible, leading Jed to label him the "six-foot stomach."

Surrounded by unforgettable characters like Miss Hathaway and Milburn Drysdale, the Clampett clan forged their way into television history, stretching from the fall of 1962 to the spring of 1971. As they did, critics from coast to coast sharpened their pencils and their tongues. They labeled them everything from a "desert in television's vast wasteland" to "painful to sit through." One critic, however, tempered his tone. *TV Guide's* Gilbert Seldes noted, "The whole notion on which *The Beverly Hillbillies* is founded is an encouragement to ignorance." Then he added, "But it is *funny.* What can I do?"

Evading the "Human Hounds"

Frederick Douglas's dramatic flight to freedom

"Minutes were hours, and hours were days," Frederick Douglas reflected in a memoir. He was reliving his daring 1838 escape through the proslavery states of Maryland and Delaware. He had already pulled off the gutsy maneuver of fooling a train conductor, but knew peril lurked down the track. As the train pulled near the Delaware border, Frederick's senses took in every sight and sound. He knew that slave-catchers, whom he described as "human hounds," awaited their prey in the border areas. "The heart of no fox or deer with hungry hounds on his tail in full chase," he declared, "could have beaten more anxiously or noisily than did mine from the time I left Baltimore, until I reached Philadelphia."

Frederick prayed his good fortune would hold out until he reached the free state of Pennsylvania. It had to be wearing thin, he surmised, since it had already saved him from near disaster with the conductor. He knew that many Baltimore residents had a soft spot for sailors because their city was a seaport. With the indispensible help of a local free black woman, Anna Murray, Frederick had obtained a makeshift sailor outfit and was provided with some money for his escape. During their planning, the relationship began to take on a romantic aspect. Although he had no "free papers" to prove he was a freeman, he had managed to borrow a friend's *sailor's protection* document, which allowed free passage from port to port.

Through several years of slavery, he had toiled among sailors on the Baltimore docks. This experience would prove invaluable to him. "I knew a ship from stem to stern and from keelson to cross-trees," he reflected, "and could talk sailor like an *old salt.*" Despite his inner turmoil, Frederick managed to assume a casual self-possessed stance as the train conductor approached. His sailor garb brought a slight smile to the conductor's face. In a friendly tone, the conductor inquired, "I suppose you have your free papers?"

"No sir," Frederick responded with as much of a cocky sailor attitude as he could muster, "I never carry my free papers to sea with me." The conductor nodded in understanding and asked if he had something else to show he was a freeman. Frederick calmed his trembling hands and produced his friend's sailor's protection paper. The American eagle on the paper's formal letterhead seemed to do the trick. The satisfied conductor took the fare and continued walking. "Had the conductor looked closely at the paper," Frederick later revealed, "he could not have failed to discover that it called for a very different looking person from myself..." Since he was mixed race, with a black mother and white father, he was of a considerably lighter complexion than his sailor friend. Incidentally, although he said "the opinion was whispered that my master was my father," this was never confirmed.

As his exhilarating but nerve-wracking day continued, on the third of September in 1838, destiny was slowly cracking open the door for one of the most famous Civil Rights leaders of all time. He breathed a well-earned sigh of relief as the train rolled on toward potential freedom, but Frederick knew well that he had only passed the first of many trials. He soon recognized a German blacksmith he knew well. The man looked intently at Frederick, stirring terror inside him. "I really believe he knew me, but had no heart to betray me," he later conjectured. "At any rate, he saw me escaping and held his peace."

The afternoon of the next day, Frederick reached Wilmington, Delaware where he boarded a steamship bound for Philadelphia. Although Pennsylvania was a free state, Frederick wanted to lose himself in the bustling impersonal atmosphere of New York, and soon took a train bound for the city. As he stepped off the train in New York, a wave of exhilaration swept over him. "I felt as one might feel upon escape from a den of hungry lions," he enthused in a letter to a friend. "Anguish and grief, like darkness and rain, may be depicted; but gladness and joy, like the rainbow, defy the skill of pen or pencil."

His elation, however, was soon stifled. He ran into a fellow fugitive he had known as a slave back in Baltimore. The man told Frederick that New York was full of slave-catchers. In fact, he said that many other blacks might betray him for only a few dollars' bounty. He must not go to the wharves to look for work, or into any colored boarding houses, he warned, since such places were closely watched. Frederick later noted that his nervous companion even seemed to fear that *he* might be a spy. "Under this apprehension, as I suppose, he showed signs of wishing to be rid of me." Alone again, Frederick summarized his dismal situation. He was "indeed free – from slavery, but free from food and shelter as well." "Every door," he concluded," seemed closed against me."

Out of desperation, he decided to confide his secret to one more person. He noticed a sailor on Centre Street who seemed to have an honest demeanor. Fortunately, Frederick's first impression proved correct, and after the sailor learned of his predicament, he took him to his home to rest for the night. The next morning, they both traveled to see an Underground Railroad officer named David Ruggles. This meeting would open the doors that had previously been sealed. Ruggles was the secretary of the New York Vigilance Committee, an antislavery organization, which assisted fugitive slaves. "I was hidden several days," Frederick related, "during which time my intended wife (Anna) came on from Baltimore at my call."

When Ruggles learned that Frederick was an expert at caulking ships, he decided that New Bedford, Massachusetts with its robust whaling trade should be Frederick and Anna's new home. On the day of their marriage, they set off for their new life there. They were taken in by a benevolent couple, Nathan and Mary Johnson. Even though New Bedford was a solid antislavery town, Frederick decided he should select a new last name, since he was known as Frederick Bailey during his slave days. He asked Nathan to choose a name for him.

Nathan had just enjoyed reading Walter Scott's poem, *The Lady of the Lake*. Since two of the characters in the poem had the surname of Douglas, he suggested the name. Adding an "s," Frederick coined the name that would be forever inscribed in Civil Rights history.

Douglass's experiences with his helpful white neighbors in New Bedford, as well as his awareness that some of New York blacks conspired against members of their own race, convinced him that good and bad come in all colors. The motto of his soon-to-be-famous abolitionist newspaper, *The North Star*, highlighted this belief. From its 1847 conception, the paper's banner stated, "Right is of no Sex – Truth is of no Color – God is the father of us all, and we are all brethren." Through his successful newspaper, as well as hundreds of speaking engagements, and three memoirs, Douglass gave voice to the aspirations of millions of enslaved souls.

During his long and productive life, Frederick Douglass was the most celebrated black man of his era. He was also the most photographed American of any race in the 1800's. Drawing upon his early love of words, and an ability to read and write obtained covertly from white children, he quickly became a master of the art of discourse. In fact, a review of an early speech he gave at the Massachusetts Anti-slavery Society's annual meeting, foretold his rhetorical success. "Flinty hearts were pierced," the admiring correspondent reported, "and cold ones melted by his eloquence."

THOSE CLEVER SIGNS
ALONG THE WAY
THAT NEVER FAILED TO
MAKE OUR DAY

Those great old Burma Shave signs

"It was a good way to starve to death fast," Clinton Odell recalled. He was reflecting on the days when he and his sons, Leonard and Alan, peddled their products door-to-door. Their first homegrown concoction, Burma-Vita Liniment, was advertised as containing ingredients from the "Malay Peninsula and Burma." Other than providing the impetus for their company's name, though, it didn't do much else for them. Their little family business, the Odells decided, simply had to expand to include another product.

They hired a chemist to concoct their latest innovation – a brushless shaving cream that could be sold in jars and tubes. In 1925, that new addition, Burma Shave, was ready to be introduced to the public. Unfortunately, the public was not particularly interested in meeting it. After all, men had been whisking up a warm foaming cup of shaving suds with their badger-hair brushes for years. In fact, most had their own special shaving mug.

If the Odells were going to sell their new brushless miracle, they would have to come up with a clever sales strategy. But one after another, their schemes fell flat. Their "Jars on Approval" concept hadn't taken off at all. The Odell boys knocked on office doors around their hometown of Minneapolis, handing out free jars of the product. The men in the office were told that if they liked it, they could pay the 50-cent cost later. If not, they could give back the unused portion and would "remain friends." Too often, their new *friends* simply used up the jar and didn't get around to either paying for it or ordering another.

Then, there was the time the Odells handed out free tubes of Burma Shave to fans entering New York's Ebbets Field. All went well as the fans inspected their newfound gifts. Then suddenly, the advertising campaign shattered. An umpire made an unpopular call against the home crowd's beloved Dodgers. Apparently the angry fans wanted to see how good a *dodger* the ump was, because the air was soon filled with little Burma Shave missiles. No, the Odells definitely needed to devise a more successful promotion.

That would come in the fall of 1925 when Alan noticed a service station's advertising signs. Unlike most businesses, which displayed one large sign, they had stretched their message across several smaller ones. He first read "gas," then "oil," followed by "restrooms," and finally a small sign with an arrow pointing to the gas station. Suddenly, something clicked in Alan's creative little brain. Even though he wasn't looking for a service station, the series of signs had held his attention to the end. He wondered if that same concept might boost sales for his family's new product. Later that day, he excitedly pitched the idea to his father.

Regrettably, his father's reaction didn't match his own enthusiasm. Clinton wrinkled his brow and shook his head. It would just cost too much, he declared, to rent all the separate spaces from the local farmers in order to put up sets of signs. He didn't see why one large one wouldn't work just as well. Undaunted, Alan explained his theory that the string of signs would hold the traveler's interest for a longer time.

Still reluctant, his father eventually agreed to give him $200 to try out his new scheme. Alan and Leonard set to work buying used boards and cutting them into 36-inch lengths. After painting them red, they wrote basic advertising copy in large white capital letters on each consecutive sign. The messages were straight forward advertisements. One series noted: SHAVE THE MODERN WAY; FINE FOR THE SKIN; DRUGGISTS HAVE IT; Burma Shave.

Rushing to put up their signs before the ground froze; the brothers installed several sets along both Highway 61 and Highway 65, leading out of Minneapolis. Then, they sat back and waited. They didn't have to wait long before orders began to pour in. The next year, they spread their signs out to include Minnesota and Wisconsin. By the end of the year, the previously lackluster Burma Shave annual sales reached $68,000. The next year, 1927, the company's sales climbed to $135,000. Clearly, the signs were doing their jobs. The following year would mark the beginning of their rise toward Americana super-star status. The signs' messages, now spreading across America, were not only promotional, they were *funny* as well.

And so, the era of Burma Shave sign humor was off and running. One sign set told us BEN MET ANNA; MADE A HIT; NEGLECTED BEARD; BEN-ANNA SPLIT; Burma Shave. Another group warned us, in a typically catchy manner, of the inherent danger in train crossings: TRAIN APPROACHING; WHISTLE SQUEALING; PAUSE, AVOID; THAT RUNDOWN FEELING. And another series warned of the potential hazard to romance of not maintaining a clean-shaven face: SHE EYED HIS BEARD; AND SAID NO DICE; THE WEDDINGS OFF; I'LL COOK THE RICE.

Year by year, the rows of signs became an integral part of the American landscape. As vacationing families scanned the monotonous panorama, someone in the back seat would squeal "Burma Shave signs!" Then came the occasionally contentious appointment of the family reader. The children often took turns reciting them aloud, which would sometimes elicit the whining complaint of "It is *too* my turn!" Clever parents would circumvent this confrontation by urging their kids to read them in unison. Someone was frequently assigned the job of looking back to read the signs on the opposite side of the road in reverse, while the family code-breakers unscrambled the message.

The highway verses vied for inclusion in the *family favorites* listing. Some voted for: THE ANSWER TO; A

MAIDEN'S PRAYER; IS NOT A CHIN; OF STUBBY HAIR. Others preferred SAID JULIET; TO ROMEO; IF YOU WON'T SHAVE; GO HOMEO. Still others selected: WITHIN THIS VALE; OF TOIL AND SIN; YOUR HEAD GROWS BALD; BUT NOT YOUR CHIN.

With tongue in cheek, the company once put up a set of signs announcing: FREE – FREE; A TRIP TO MARS; FOR 900; EMPTY JARS. Aware that it was a joke, Appleton, Wisconsin grocery store owner, Arlyss French, nevertheless decided to transform the offer into his own local publicity campaign. He got the word out to his customers that he needed their empty Burma Shave jars so he and his family could "travel to Mars." To add spice to the promotion, he displayed a simulated rocket outside the grocery and had neighborhood kids act as *little green men* on the roof and shoot toy rocket gliders into the parking lot.

When French wrote to Burma Shave to ask where he should send the jars, the Odells responded, "If a trip to Mars you'd earn, remember, friend, there's no return." Eventually, though, he did send the 900 jars to them. In a mutually beneficial promotional event, they sent Mr. French and his family on a vacation to Moers (pronounced "Mars") Germany. In keeping with the theme of the occasion, Mr. French showed up for the trip wearing a silver space suit complete with a bubble helmet. The company provided him with extra jars of Burma Shave, so he could "barter with the Martians."

It wasn't only the Odells who came up with the catchy verses. Early on, they realized the need for assistance in entertaining travelers. They organized annual jingle contests that offered a $100 prize for any they used. Before the signs faded from the landscape in the 1960s – primarily due to the advent of Interstate highways with higher speed limits, they received as many as 15,000 entries a year. Many ended up along the nation's roadsides… as well as in this chapter, because:
I THOUGHT THEIR STORY; JUST WOULDN'T FAIL; TO MAKE A "HISTORY MAKER'S" TALE.

"Norma Jean, the Human Bean"

The erratic youth of Marilyn Monroe

The teenage assembly-line worker brushed her curly ash blonde hair aside to flash a smile at the Army photographer. As she did, she left a smudge on her face from her dust-coated hands. That was okay. After all, it's not like anyone was likely to look at the picture anyway. On that 1945 summer day, the photographer had been snapping shots of nearly all the women on the assembly line. Hers would simply blend in with the others.

The Missouri-born picture taker, David Conover, had been assigned to Van Nuys, California's Radioplane Corporation plant to capture military-magazine photos of attractive assembly-line girls. The pictures were intended to boost the morale of the male soldiers in combat. Norma Jean Dougherty didn't consider herself as one of the "attractive girls" at the plant. Although she now filled out her company overalls quite well, she vividly remembered that just a few years previously, boys teased her about her skinny frame. She could still remember them chanting "Norma Jean, the Human Bean" as she passed.

Once Conover took her picture, she continued attaching propellers and spraying a plastic coating on the small airplanes. The little radio-controlled planes were used by the military as targets during anti-aircraft practice. After he finished the photo shoot, he retraced his steps and introduced himself.

"I'm Norma Jean Dougherty," she responded, as she summoned a sparkling smile and offered her hand.

"She was beautiful," Conover later told a magazine reporter. "Half child, half woman – her eyes held something that touched and intrigued me." He arranged a photo shoot for her lunch hour. After she had wiped the smudges off her face and donned a sweater from her locker, she began to pose for Conover's camera. Suddenly, the inexperienced teenager lit up with the natural instinct of a seasoned model. Conover was so enthusiastic he could hardly hold the camera still. Norma Jean, however, being on the other side of the lens, had no inkling of the importance of the moment. "Am I really photogenic?" she inquired.

That question would be enthusiastically answered by millions of fans during the years ahead. Like the doomed little airplanes she spray painted, her career would one day soar among the clouds before it was intercepted by an overpowering force, followed by a devastating crash. Before that flight was disrupted, however, she would blaze a path across the stratosphere, gracing countless magazine covers and emblazoning her new name, Marilyn Monroe, on theater marquees around the world.

Years before that phenomenal flight, though, young Norma Jean's life journey seemed anything *but* bound for the sky. Her mother, Gladys Mortensen, worked as a film-cutter at Los Angeles's Consolidated Film Industries. She gave birth to her on June 1st, 1926, in the charity ward of Los Angeles General Hospital. Although Gladys listed her baby's father as Edward Mortenson – her divorced second husband, many biographers feel it was actually C. Stanley Griffith, one of her co-workers at the studio.

Griffith, a dapper lady's man sporting a pencil-thin mustache, made it clear to Gladys that he had no interest in playing a fatherly role. Nonetheless, Gladys bravely entered the hospital to bring her baby into the world. Smitten by Hollywood's glamour, she named her daughter after the then-popular screen idol, Norma Talmadge.

Not only did Gladys face the challenge of single-parenting, her emotional strength was shaky to begin with. Both of her parents finished their lives in mental institutions, and her brother, Marion, was diagnosed with paranoid schizophrenia. Many historians feel it was actually bipolar disorder. As if Gladys's odds of success weren't low enough, she married at sixteen and spent years in an abusive relationship before filing for divorce.

Soon, she moved to Hawthorne, a Los Angeles suburb, where her mother was living. Unfortunately, mom was preparing to leave the country to hopefully rekindle a flame with her estranged husband. Gladys made arrangements to stay in Hawthorne with Wayne and Ida Bolender, a couple who took in boarders and fostered several children. Within a couple weeks, she returned to her work at the film studio, placing Norma Jean in the care of the Bolenders, but making regular visits to see her.

By 1933, when Norma Jean was about 8-years-old, her mother was finally able to put a down payment on a little bungalow near the Hollywood Bowl, and take her daughter back. During this period, Gladys would often take her out to the movies. As the little dreamer stood in front of Grauman's Chinese theater, with her feet planted firmly in the footsteps of movie idols like Gloria Swanson and Clara Bow, she hoped to one day leave her own there.

Sadly this period was much too brief. In early 1935, Gladys's fragile emotional state devolved into madness. According to some reports, she shouted threats as she wielded a kitchen knife. Other than a few short periods, Gladys remained institutionalized for the remainder of her life. As police hauled her off to a local hospital, they also took with them, her daughter's childhood. The next few years of Norma Jean's life ricocheted between brief stays with relatives, foster families, and a couple years spent in the Lost Angeles Orphans Home Society.

Although Marilyn would later summarize this period with the poignant statement of, "I was never used to being happy," the same dreams that filled her head as she stood in the footprints in front of Graumans often helped lift her spirits. She would gaze out of the orphanage window toward the RKO Studio's water tower, renewing her dreams of stardom. Marilyn would later say that even though she knew thousands of other girls were dreaming the same dreams, she was convinced she was "dreaming the hardest."

The opening scene of her dream life was not far away as she peered out that window. It commenced with that click of the army photographer's shutter and played out through the years ahead in a dazzling collage of scenes as diverse as young Norma Jean's early life. She married a local boy, Jim Dougherty, when she was only 16, primarily to avoid going back to the orphanage. While serving in the Merchant Marines, Dougherty was sent to the Pacific.

During this time, Norma Jean encountered Conover, the Army photographer, who soon helped her find modeling jobs. As her modeling career took off, the Hollywood movie moguls began to notice her as well. Ben Lyon, a 20th Century Fox executive, decided she needed a catchier name. Putting their heads together, Norma Jean offered her mother's maiden name of Monroe while Lyon selected a name from one of his favorite Broadway stars, Marilyn Miller.

When Dougherty returned, he was adamant that she quit her modeling and acting career and conform to the then-traditional role of making his meals and ironing his shirts. As history is aware – she didn't. Instead, she quit the marriage. This, of course, would not be the last marriage she would quit. Her highly publicized unions with both Joe DiMaggio and Arthur Miller similarly ended in divorce.

Her career, like her relationships, often fell short of her childhood dreams and expectations. Despite a life-long desire to become known as a serious actress, Marilyn Monroe is better remembered as the first *Playboy* centerfold and the shapely actress standing over Manhattan's Lexington Avenue subway grating as a blast of air lifted her dress. Only seventeen-years spanned the clicking of David Conover's camera to the tragic closing scene shrouded in barbiturates and controversy. During that fleeting career, the turmoil between dreams and reality mirrored the early life of the little girl who was shuttled between foster homes and an orphanage. Just behind the iconic platinum blond with the entrancing eyes and the flaming ruby lipstick, forever lurked "Norma Jean, the Human Bean."

"Hatchetations"

The uninvited visits by the hatchet-wielding saloon smasher, Carrie Nation

"Go to Kiowa," the voice instructed "I'll stand by you." The recipient of this command knew exactly what she was being told to do – head to the saloons in nearby Kiowa, Kansas and spray the *vile hellholes* with broken glass and splashed booze. And she knew exactly who told her to do this – *God*. "I did not hear these words as other words," Carrie Nation later told an interviewer. "There was no voice, but they seemed to be spoken in my heart." She immediately sprang from her bed and set about putting God's will into action. "I got a box that would fit under my buggy seat," she said, "and every time I thought no one would see me, I went out in the yard to pick up some brickbats." As Carrie gathered the brick fragments that 1900 June day, she wrapped them in newspaper and tucked them into the box.

During the day of her Godly instructions, she cooked enough food to keep her husband, David, fed for the next couple days. She told him she planned to stay overnight with her friend, Mrs. Springer. Since Carrie had occasionally done this before, he was not suspicious of her actions. That afternoon, she headed out. "I hitched up my horse to the buggy," she noted, "and put the box of 'smashers' in."

Since she often pulled into Mrs. Springer's yard during rides, she thought her horse, Prince, might turn in without her prompting – so she gave him the reins. "If he turned in," she decided, "I would stay all night. If not, I would go to Kiowa." Prince, according to her recollection, not only trotted past her friend's driveway, but seemed to increase his speed. "I knew," Carrie deduced, "that it was God's will to go on." That evening she stayed in Kiowa with a friend and prayed throughout most of the night to steel her nerves for the next day's bar bashing.

"Men, I have come to save you from a drunkard's fate!" she blared the next morning as she burst into Dobson's Saloon. Dobson and another man gaped from behind the counter. "Get out of the way!" Carrie yelled, "I don't want to strike you but I am going to break up this den of vice." With that, she commenced the *saving* process by targeting rows of liquor bottles. When her bombardment was completed, she strode through the broken glass and hustled down the street to give two more Kioga saloons the Carrie Nation treatment.

In the third saloon, she decided to add the glass of the ornate mirror behind the bar to the pile of liquor bottle shards. The brickbat she hurled, though, didn't do the trick. Undaunted, Carrie spotted a single ball on the nearby billiard table. "I said 'Thank you God!' " she later reflected, "and picked it up and threw it." The eyes of the astonished bartender and his customers likely widen to near-billiard ball size as they witnessed the ivory missile smashing its target and showering the room with broken mirror glass. The siege of Carrie Nation had begun.

The spark that kindled that raging siege was ignited years before, by her first husband, Doctor Charles Gloyd. She first met him when her parents took him in as a boarder in their Cass County, Missouri home. Not only was the handsome young man a medical doctor, but he held young Carrie in awe of his intelligent conversation and ability to speak several languages. Despite her strict upbringing, Carrie found herself attracted to him. Then came the shocker. "He astonished me one evening by kissing me," she reflected. "I had never had a gentleman to take such a privilege, and felt shocked. I threw up my hands to my face, saying several times, 'I am ruined!' "

Ruined or not, Carrie slowly began to return his affections. "When I learned that Dr. Gloyd loved me, she confessed, "I began to love him." Her parents, however, did not share her affections for the good doctor. They had been noticing his frequent drinking bouts and realized he had a severe problem with alcohol. Carrie's mother forbade her to be alone with him. But Carrie found a way to covertly communicate with him. He had introduced her to Shakespeare and left a volume on his table. "If in the morning at breakfast," Carrie recalled, "he would manage to call the name 'Shakespeare,' then I knew there was a letter for me in its leaves."

Eventually, her parents accepted the pairing, but continued to worry. Their concern, sadly, was warranted. Gloyd was drunk at the wedding and drew few sober breaths afterward. Carrie routinely had to tell his patients he wasn't available to answer their emergency calls. Less than a year after their marriage and shortly before their daughter Charlien was born, they separated. The next year, 1869, Gloyd's cause of death was listed as "delirium tremens or from pneumonia compounded by excessive drinking." Not only did the wrecked marriage scar Carrie emotionally, but Charlien developed a number of physical and emotional concerns – which Carrie attributed to alcohol.

The ingredient in Carrie's personality that might have led to the seemingly excessive nature of her later reaction flowed through her family's bloodlines. Her grandmother on her mother's side, reportedly needed to be "kept behind bars" in her later years due to extreme behavior. Following this colorful family tradition, Carrie's mother, Mary, not only began to dress like England's Queen Victoria, but according to accounts, often believed she *was* the queen. She strolled around in a purple velvet robe, sporting a gold-colored crown adorned with a large chunk of colored cut glass. When she rode in a carriage, she forced a servant to don a red coat and gallop ahead announcing her presence with a brass trumpet. Not unpredictably, she spent her final years in a mental hospital, or "lunatic asylum" as they were then known.

Carrie's bottle breaking in Kiowa just whetted her appetite for more of the same. Her second husband, David Nation, whom she had told she was just visiting a neighbor, didn't seem particularly upset at her behavior. In fact, when he heard about her brickbat and rock throwing incidents, he lightheartedly suggested she should use a hatchet next time to cause more damage. "That's the most sensible thing you have said since I married you," she responded. With that, her modus operandi switched to smashing and bashing during what she would call her "hatchetations."

Carrie rampaged through Kansas, Missouri, and Oklahoma like a cyclone. She would line up a speech, usually at a local church, and stir many of the congregation into a prohibitionist frenzy. Later, she would lead a group into the bars, which she often referred to as "murder shops," singing hymns and sometimes joining in the hatcheting. Saloons across the Midwest soon displayed signs reading "All nations welcome but Carrie." One journalist described her as a "six-foot tall stevedore with the face of a prison warden and the persistence of a toothache."

Carrie laid down her hatchet after a couple years of smashing and twenty-three visits to local jails. She changed the spelling of her name to Carry Nation, to let folks know she intended to "*carry a nation* from the darkness of drunken bestiality into the light of purity and sobriety." She gave hundreds of prohibitionist speeches and for a while, lectured on the vaudeville circuit, often reenacting her notorious bar-bashing scenes. "I want to do what God tells me to do," she told a judge after one of her *hatchetations.* "I am commanded," she explained, "to cry aloud about sin and not to whisper about it." And as history has recorded, Carry Nation was never once accused of whispering.

The "Yankee" Voice of the South

Stephen Foster, the "father of American Music"

It's easy to picture Stephen Foster sitting "way down upon" the banks of Florida's Swanee River, transforming its rippling beauty into words and musical notes. And it is similarly easy to envision him under a vivid blue Alabama sky, breathing in the pine-scented air as he wrote about a traveler with a *banjo on his knee*. As tambourines, banjos, and rhythmic *bones* backed up harmonic voices, his songs almost smelled of magnolia blossoms. Stephen Foster seems to have been the true *voice of the South*. The only thing is – he never lived there. The only time the northern songwriter ever went south of the Mason-Dixon Line was during a honeymoon steamboat trip to New Orleans. But that was okay; he had the soul of a southerner.

It's not as if he was the only "Yankee" to write southern standards. Ohio native, Daniel Emmett, wrote "Dixie" in a New York City hotel room. Emmett, a staunch Union supporter, was appalled when he learned the Confederacy began using "Dixie" as a rallying call. "If I had known to what use they were going to put my song," he complained to a friend, "I will be damned if I'd have written it!" But he probably couldn't have stopped himself. After all, there was just something about the relaxed southern lifestyle that produced a nostalgic yearning in northern songwriters to return – even if they had never been there.

Stephen Foster's life would probably have turned out better if he *were* born in the South. He might have strolled down the grassy lanes and leaned back against the shade trees he envisioned in his songs. He likely wouldn't have ended up dying at the age of 37 in a Bowery flop house with only 38-cents to his name. Yes, during his abbreviated life, the man often cited as "the father of American music" fell from the lofty perch of national acclaim into the valley of near obscurity. Chronic destitution haunted him during a life marred with marital

172

problems and alcoholism. He valiantly fought with music publishers throughout his life to squeeze a few more pennies out of his songs, as those publishers made a fortune from them. As it turned out, Stephen Foster was not only America's first fulltime professional songwriter – he was also the first one to be victimized by the greedy music industry.

The opening scenes of his life belied the stressful ending. He was surrounded by music in his family's stately Pennsylvania home. His sisters harmonized around the family piano to the latest sentimental "parlor songs." On Sundays, the family's housekeeper, Olivia Pise, took Stephen to her church where the soulful black gospel sounds shook the walls. In addition, minstrel show songs strongly influenced him, since the shows were wildly popular when he was growing up. As the diverse styles molded his musical taste, his natural abilities blossomed. He soon taught himself to play nearly every instrument he came in contact with. His family members recalled him picking out tunes on a guitar at the age of two, and at seven, piping out a perfect melody in a music store on a flute-type instrument called a *flageolet.*

He and his brother Morrison joined with some close friends to form a little boy's club they called the Knights of the S. T. History has lost the meaning of S. T., but it was most likely "square table" as opposed to the Knights of the Round Table. They met periodically at the Foster home where they often sang the popular tunes of the day for his family. Not satisfied with simply using existing material, Stephen began to write new songs for them to sing. One of these, according to most music historians, was "Oh! Susanna." The title likely stemmed from his sister Charlotte Susanna Foster's middle name. The little harmonizing group of buddies likely had no idea that folks would still be singing it over a hundred-and-fifty years later.

Stephen wrote a number of songs as a teen, but there was just something special about the bouncy "Oh! Susanna." The first public performance of the song came in September of 1847 at Andrew's Eagle Ice Cream Saloon in Pittsburgh. The little second-floor ice cream parlor had begun offering entertainment to attract customers for their ice cream and confections. The ten-cent admission fee for the show was waved if they ordered dessert. As a local quintet sang from the sheet music Stephen's brother, Morrison, had provided them, the place came alive.

The song would soon be joined by other popular numbers as Foster turned his energy toward his songwriting. The following year, "Oh! Susanna" came out in a song-sheet format, and in 1850, "Nelly Bly," "Angelina Baker," and "Nelly Was a Lady" joined the list. He also wrote a novelty song that year about a racetrack near his Pennsylvania home called the Camptown Races. The "Doo-da, Doo-da" in the catchy lyrics would eventually work its way into popular culture. Although many people nowadays frown at the mention of Stephen Foster's name due to racial sensitivity, he was actually viewed at the time, as being rather progressive since his song referred to an African American woman as a "lady." The term, back then, was usually reserved for well-to-do white women.

Foster knew that two main musical genres were open to his songs – the popular sentimental parlor songs, which sold by the hundreds of thousands of copies on song sheets, and the bouncy or soulful minstrel show songs that filled nearly every opera house across the country. Most opera houses, incidentally, never hosted an opera – the name just had a cultural flair. He began handing out the sheet music of his newly written songs to minstrel performers as they played in nearby theaters.

In 1849, he negotiated a contract with New York's Firth & Pond song-sheet publishers, and the next year, met with E. P. Christy, the leader of the popular Christy Minstrels. Foster included a stipulation in his contract with Christy. His songs, he instructed, should not be sung in a condescending manner like most minstrel songs of the day. Rather, he told Christy, they were designed to elicit compassion for the characters in his songs, "instead of the trashy and really offensive words which belong to some songs of that order." In addition, he soon stopped writing them in the derogatory black dialect most songwriters continued to use. In fact "My Old Kentucky Home" and "Old Folks at Home" were often used in theatrical performances of the anti-slavery story, *Uncle Tom's Cabin.*

Although he yearned to become a full-time songwriter, he worked several years as a bookkeeper for his brother's steamship company. The lure of marketing musical notes and words eventually overcame the security of calculating rows of numbers. When he signed up with the music publishing company and the minstrel show manager, he cut himself free of the bookkeeping position and sailed into the unknown waters of freelance songwriting.

Unfortunately, those waters could get pretty choppy in the days before performing rights organizations like ASCAP and BMI came along. He sold most of his songs for a lump sum payment. That *lump*, incidentally, was usually pretty miniscule. "Oh Suzanna," for example, brought him a whopping one hundred bucks. Sometimes, if he really pushed it, Foster could squeeze out a couple of pennies royalties for each copy of sheet music sold by publishers. The constant money battles likely played a major part in stirring the clouds of gloom which often loomed over his life and his troubled marriage. Sadly the peaceful strains of his "Beautiful Dreamer" and "Jeanie with the Light Brown Hair" didn't furnish the background music to his life as much as his mournful "Hard Times Come Again No More."

When the Bands Got Big

The fabulous "Big Band era"

Where was everybody? Benny knew a lot of folks out there in *radioland* loved his music. All the telegraphs and letters he had received made that crystal clear. In order to meet them, he had booked a tour beginning in New York City and ending with a three-week gig at the Palomar Ballroom in Los Angeles. But as he glumly surveyed the dance floor in the mid-western ballroom, Benny Goodman experienced the same sinking feeling he had in the east coast venues. The bandstand looked great, the microphones worked perfectly, and his band members had practiced until they could deliver the swinging melodies with a sparkle. But where were the enthusiastic dancers who had swooned over his band's new sound on the radio?

He could still remember his exhilaration when the NBC radio executives informed him that his emerging band had nabbed a spot on their new dance-band show, "Let's Dance." The program started at 10:30 p.m. and continued for the next three hours, featuring various groups playing in 15-minute intervals. Unfortunately, Goodman's band usually played near the end of the show. That was okay, though, they were *on the airwaves*!

If Benny Goodman had noticed the addresses on the congratulatory letters and telegraphs that flooded the NBC studios, he could have solved the mystery of the nearly empty eastern and mid-western ballrooms. The comments nearly all came from the west coast! The teenagers in the East and Midwest weren't allowed to stay up late enough on school nights to take in Benny's new Swing sound. But with the 3-hour time change, the California teens had plenty of time to tune in, swoon, and dance before bedtime.

Finally, in California, the mysterious fans appeared. At Oakland's McFadden's Ballroom, the band was met by a good-sized crowd of youngsters who cheered the songs they had been hearing on Let's Dance. Then, two nights later, August 21st, 1935, the real test occurred – the first night of a three-week engagement in Los Angeles at the Palomar Ballroom. They were greeted by a sizeable crowd but the standard arrangements they played during their first set, didn't create much excitement. Goodman's enthusiasm, stirred up by the Oakland crowd, began to dissipate. After all, he knew the Palomar represented the chance of a lifetime. Not only was the venue already legendary, but the show was broadcast on national radio. Benny would likely have given the dancers back the forty cents they had each plunked down to enter – if only they would show a little more *pizzazz*!

During their break, according to their booking agent's recollections, drummer Gene Krupa told Goodman they should begin the set with their own songs. "If we're gonna die, Benny," Krupa advised, "Let's die playing our own thing." Music history has confirmed the value of Krupa's suggestion. The place erupted as the first few spirited notes of the new Swing sound flew out of their instruments. The vibrant arrangements by Fletcher Henderson and Spud Murphy ignited the dancers. The "Swing" music era was officially launched.

Nowadays some people use the terms Swing era and Big Band era interchangeably. Actually, though, many bands had already swelled in size by the time Swing-dance craze swept the nation. Ironically, this was partially the result of the crippling depression. Shrinking wages for musicians let band leaders hire a dozen or more players. Despite the economic ravages of the period, many people managed to scrape together a dime or two to spend a few hours in their local nightclubs and ballrooms. As they did, the trumpets, trombones, and saxophones worked their wonders – replacing their blues with *their own* blues, as well as jazz and dance tunes.

The roots of many of those tunes reach back to the birthplace of Jazz – New Orleans. Many striving musicians there in the 1890s, bought used instruments from decommissioned military bands of the Spanish American War. Since many taught themselves how to play, their music sometimes had an unconventional sound. Ragtime, for example, was influenced by early African American banjo styles, which emphasized an "offbeat" syncopation. This is also a common element in the Blues, which similarly flavored the New Orleans musical recipe. As the bubbling mixture of Jazz, Blues, Ragtime, and dance music permeated the southern dance clubs during the teens and twenties, several factors combined to thrust it across the nation in the 1930s.

For one thing, radio had already sailed through the airwaves into millions of living rooms. The new entertainment was priced perfectly for the depression area – *free.* Some stations began to include recorded discs of known bands, in addition to local live entertainment. The sound quality of the recordings vastly improved in 1931 with the introduction of RCA's "Velocity" microphone. The subtle tones of the muted horns and velvety singers were picked up by the sensitive mikes. A couple years later, Homer Capehart sold his "Simplex record changer mechanism" to a New York piano and organ manufacturing company started by Rudolph Wurlitzer. They had already produced coin-operated pianos and phonographs, and shortly their Wurlitzer "jukeboxes" spread the new music to cafes and bars across America.

As the excited public strolled into the ballrooms, tuned through the radio static, or slid their nickels down a jukebox slot, they developed favorite big bands. One of their favorite Jazz style bands was headed by William Basie. After several years with other groups, he worked his way into the top-rated Bennie Moten Band in Kansas City. Williams said that he was guilty of sometimes slipping off during arranging sessions, leaving Moten to ask the band, "Where is that no 'count rascal?"

178

That was the genesis, he noted, of his famous nickname "Count Basie."

Another name that became a favorite was Dorsey. Tommy and Jimmy Dorsey came from the little coal-mining town of Shenandoah, Pennsylvania where their father fueled their musical interests. Thomas Dorsey was initially a coal miner, but had improved his lot – teaching music and heading his own band. He wanted his sons to escape the mining life too and pushed music as their potential future occupations. To assure they practiced their instruments, he hid their shoes so they wouldn't sneak outside to play. Apparently Pennsylvania kids don't play barefoot. His scheme paid off and the Dorsey Brothers, both individually and together, carved their name deep into Big Band history.

Of course it's impossible to discuss the Big Band era without mentioning the Glenn Miller orchestra. Although he looked more like a staid school teacher than a bandleader, Miller's music could bring shivers and even tears to his fans. His button-down persona didn't reflect it, but he was a mid-western farm boy. In fact, Glenn bought his first trombone with the money he made from milking cows. He religiously practiced hour after hour. His mother later reflected that, "it got to where Pop and I used to wonder if he'd ever amount to anything." Of course, they had nothing to worry about. Before we lost him in 1944, his band had racked up 17 number-one singles plus 59 top-ten hits – more than Elvis and the Beatles combined would later collect.

The spotlight of musical history shined on the Big Bands for only a decade, from the mid 30s to the mid 40s. It glared so brightly, however, it seared its images deep into the hearts of its fans. Their eyes still sparkle while they recall the rollicking sounds of Les Brown and his "Band of Renown" or Woody Herman and "Herman's Herd." The same eyes sometimes mist up with the reflections of holding their dates tight to swing and sway with Sammy Kaye or glide along the dance floor to Guy Lombardo's "sweetest music this side of heaven." Those eyes, in fact, often begin to gleam with the mere mention of the Big Band era.

"The Saint of the Gutter"

Mother Teresa, the irrepressible spirit who served
Calcutta's unwanted, uncared for, and unloved

"When you do good," the young girl's mother instructed,
"do it quietly, as if you were throwing a stone into the sea." As
the little bright-eyed Albanian girl took in her words, she
carefully stored them in her memory alongside the other
lessons she had previously bestowed. "My child," her mother
once told her as they sat in their little three-room mud-brick
home, "never eat a single mouthful unless you are sharing it
with others."

She often embodied both lessons as she quietly
extended dinner invitations to her destitute neighbors in their
little Macedonian town. One reason her daughter listened so
attentively to her lessons, was the awareness that she not only
spoke them, she lived them. What a beautiful thing it would be,
little Gondzha, daydreamed, if she could one day live them as
her mother did.

Not only would Gondzha live out her dreams to "do
good," she would also live up to her name, which in Albanian
means "bud" or "rosebud." As she matured and flowered, she
would eventually wrap her comforting petals around thousands
of the "poorest of the poor." Her own words, like those she so
often heard in childhood, would later inspire not only reflection
and meditation, but action and involvement. The multitudes that
would one day revere and follow her, did so for the same reason
she had cherished her mother – they knew her words and her
actions were one and the same.

Gondzha, who would eventually be known around the
world as "Mother Teresa," developed a unique ability to distil
her beliefs into easily understood principles. When stressing
the need to build a hospice for the dying in the Calcutta slums,
for example, she observed, "A beautiful death is for people who

lived like animals, to die like angels." In explaining her commitment to working with victims of Leprosy, she stated, "I wouldn't touch a leper for a thousand pounds; yet I willingly cure him for the love of God." And when told there were simply "too many children" in poverty for her to make a difference, she responded from the heart. "How can you say there are too many children? That's like saying there are too many flowers!"

Despite the growing world-wide recognition of her words and deeds, she felt she was simply "a little pencil in the hand of a writing God, who is sending a love letter to the world." This humility stemmed deep from her heart. Her eventual legion of admirers agreed with nearly all of Mother's Teresa's statements, but often disputed her humble self-assessment. Speaking for millions, Cardinal Pietro Parolin once referred to her as a "gleaming mirror of God's love." And when the United Nations secretary-general, Javier Perez de Cuellar, reflected on her ability to spread peace among hostile nations, he enthused, "she is the United Nations."

Long before this international acclaim, the little Albanian girl was forced to face a life-changing loss at the tender age of eight. Without warning, her father, Nikola, became suddenly stricken and died. Prior to his death, he had become active in community politics, and was quite vocal in his support of Albanian independence. Because of this, many locals felt his death was the result of poisoning by his political rivals. As a result of losing her father, Gondzha became very close to her mother. She also focused intently on her studies and her music. Her beautiful soprano voice often added a delightful harmony to her Sacred Heart choir.

Another interest began to blossom early in her life – listening to tales of her church's missionaries, springing from their service in foreign countries. In addition to enjoying their accounts, she read letters of Jesuit missionaries and nuns who worked with impoverished people in India. When she was 12, as she would later recall, she decided she had been "born with a desire to go and help the poor in India." As dreams of her future began to include visions of serving India's poor and downtrodden, she became convinced that she should follow her religious inclinations.

Although she began spending much of her time in church-related activities with her youth group, she didn't consider becoming a nun. That decision came when she was 18 in 1928, following what she said was a calling from God. He had instructed her, she later reflected, that she had many talents and "must use them for people who need help in the world and to love and care for them." In response, she decided to leave home and join the Sisters of Loreto in Dublin, Ireland, since they had a missionary program in India.

Though her family and friends admired her strength of will, they were sad about her departure. Her youth group met her at the train station and gave her a personal concert. One of her close friends, Lawrence Anthony, recalled the event years later. After the concert, which she also joined, Anthony and her other friends stood at the station until the train arrived. "Gondzha gave me a photograph and laughed. 'Here,' she said, 'this will be your last memento of Gondzha.' " Then, on that September day, after sad goodbyes, she boarded a train for Dublin, leaving her friends and family forever. Although she had promised not to cry, tears streamed down her cheeks as the train pulled away and she steadily waved as her friends slowly disappeared.

During her year with Dublin's Sisters of Loreta, Gondzha learned English in preparation for a teaching position. There, she took the name Sister Mary Teresa, after Saint Therese of Lisieux, the patron saint of missionaries. Since a nun in the convent had had already chosen that name, she took the Spanish spelling, Teresa. Late in 1928, she departed for Calcutta, India, arriving early the next year. Following further study, she was assigned to teach at St. Mary's High School for girls. The next 15 years found the young sister happily teaching history and geography to the daughters of Calcutta's affluent Catholic citizens. Despite her enjoyment of her career, those

183

earlier visions of helping the poor flashed before her eyes every time she passed by the slums of the city. She simply couldn't block out the visions of the desperate faces and vacant eyes that returned her gaze.

Those faces continued to haunt her thoughts during an annual retreat to Darjeeling. As she gazed out the window of the train in September of 1946, she received a second calling – or as she would later phrase it, "a call within a call." Suddenly, in a way she never described, Jesus revealed his disappointment and pain to her regarding the neglect of the poor. During the calling, she felt the need to build a religious community to bring service to the poorest of the poor. She would call it The Missionaries of Charity. After nearly two years of planning and pleading, she received permission from the church hierarchy to begin her new endeavor. On a hot August morning, she set out from her comfortable Loreto convent, wearing a blue-bordered white sari, to enter the world of absolute poverty.

The often-told history of Mother Teresa's remaining decades traces her path from scratching words in the dirt in her outdoor classroom, to overseeing more than 600 missions in over 120 countries. Along that pathway to world-wide renown and eventual sainthood, she maintained the spirit of that little girl who loved to sing and hear the missionaries' stories. As time etched wrinkles into her once-smooth face, it left one part alone – the sparkle in her loving eyes. Those eyes and that sparkle still inspire millions as they gaze at pictures of the character-filled face of Mother Teresa, lovingly called the Saint of the Gutter.

The Queen of Variety

The Inimitable Carol Burnett

Early on, several television *gurus* had informed Carol Burnett she was simply "too loud and too big" to make it as a TV comedian. Fortunately, she was soon able to prove them wrong by popping in on millions of Americans every week during the run of the popular Garry Moore Show. If their little TV screens had two-way vision, her tiny black-and-white character could have peered back at those fans. She would have seen typically staid bankers, librarians, and school teachers, all wiping away tears of laughter over her goofball expressions and slapstick antics. The rave reviews and shining Emmy award she garnered during the show's run, helped to quell the critics of her incomparable brash comedic style.

Now, though, the naysayers were back again – this time to squelch her dream of stepping into the spotlight as a variety show host. That position, they informed her, was a "man's game." Although Dinah Shore had cracked opened the door a decade before, the popular variety show hosts of the day like Ed Sullivan, Sid Caesar, Dean Martin, and the rest, all had one thing in common – they were men. The CBS executives had no problem with giving Carol her own show. After all, she was hilarious, and the contract she had signed with them included a "push the button" stipulation.

If within five years of signing, she wanted her own show, she simply had to *push the button* by asking for it. After the Garry Moore Show wrapped up, she decided to take them up on the offer. "Great," they responded; they had a situation comedy called "Here's Agnes" that would be ideal for her. She appreciated their enthusiasm, but a situation comedy had never been Carol's dream. She had always enjoyed variety shows when she was young, and had loved being part of Moore's program. There was just something about the variety format that fit her perfectly. It was time, she concluded, to stand her ground against the CBS *suits*. Somehow she had to get them to share her vision of a successful intruder into the "man's game" of variety hosts – *her!*

Her gentle but firm confrontation likely left the network executives wondering what had just happened. Although they had previously stood firmly behind their "men-only" criteria, they found themselves offering Carol a contract to produce 30 one-hour episodes of her very own variety show. Not only that, but they ended up giving her nearly total control over the production. *What had happened,* incidentally, was that they had just encountered the incomparable gust of charm, fortitude, humor, and insight that would blast through the next decade like a comedic hurricane – Carol Burnett.

The first puff of that future humor-storm stirred when Carol was in the second grade. She invented an imaginary twin sister she named Karen. Soon, young Carol decided to introduce her to the neighbors. Carol would make an appearance as Karen, then step inside their house and frantically change clothes to reappear through another door as herself. She enjoyed the ruse for awhile, but as Carol later recalled, "I became exhausted and Karen mysteriously disappeared."

The laughs she secretly relished helped to momentarily brighten a childhood too often cast in shadows by the alcoholism of both of her mother and father. Predictably, her parents' relationship soon collapsed. Following their legal separation when Carol was eight, she was raised by her maternal grandmother in a small studio apartment in Hollywood. Her grandmother, Mabel, or "Nanny" as Carol would always call her, was a loving and feisty character who instilled a love of movies in her granddaughter by taking her to see their silver-screen heroes almost every night. They became very close, and Nanny developed a little secret signal to remind Carol she loved her – she gave a little tug on her left ear. Many years later, this ear tug would become a clandestine signal back to her of Carol's love, given at the end of every Carol Burnett Show.

Another signature element of her show, the Tarzan yell, also traces back to her childhood. As early as nine, she began to rattle the walls with her version of the jungle man's unique communication technique. Many years later, this rare skill would not only send viewers into fits of laughter, but would once get her out of trouble; then plunge her into even deeper trouble. She was running late for a rehearsal in New York and realized she needed to buy a pair of stockings. Quickly stepping inside the posh Bergdorf Goodman department store, she selected a pair and headed toward the register. Along the way, a sales lady recognized her and asked for autographs for her five grandchildren. Despite her hurry, Carol graciously complied.

When she arrived at the register, Carol realized she had put the wrong wallet in her purse and didn't have her credit cards or identification. She did have a checkbook and asked the same saleslady if she could write a check. Obviously she recognized Carol, since she previously asked for autographs, but she nervously informed her that store policy required a picture ID. Sheepishly, she summoned the manager to see what to do. Taking advantage of an opportunity, the manager recognized Carol, but firmly declared the only way they could be sure of her identify was if she would do the Tarzan yell. Playing along with the gag, Carol reared back and let her fly. Suddenly the door behind the manager flew open to reveal a security guard with his gun drawn. "Now," Carol reflected with a twinkle in her eye, "I only do the yell in controlled circumstances."

Carol's love of movies, which Nanny helped ignite, led to one of her first jobs – that of an usherette at Hollywood's Warner Brothers' Theater. Her position, however, wasn't long lasting. When a couple arrived five minutes before the surprise ending of Alfred Hitchcock's "Strangers on a Train," Carol asked them to wait until the movie was over to avoid spoiling the suspense for them. They insisted, however, on being seated. Seeing his new usherette resisting their entry into the theater, the manager strode forward and not only fired Carol, but unceremoniously ripped the epaulettes from her uniform to emphasize his point. Years later, when Carol was given a star on the Hollywood Walk of Fame, she asked that it be placed directly in front of the old Warner Brothers' Theater, in order to belatedly *emphasize her point.*

The years of wonderful acting that led to that star, might not have transpired if it weren't for an academic requirement Carol wasn't exactly happy about. Writing was actually her goal, likely because of her mother's job as a successful movie studio publicity writer before the alcohol took control. Carol enrolled in the University of California in Los Angeles, majoring first in journalism, then in theater arts and English. One of the requirements of entering a playwright program at the college was to attend an acting workshop. She reluctantly enrolled in the workshop, but soon fell in love with the acting profession.

After getting laughs during her first performance, Carol was hooked. "All of a sudden, after so much coldness and emptiness in my life," she would later recall, "I knew the sensation of all that warmth wrapping around me." During the decades to follow, she would wrap her own warmth around millions of admirers. As those fans later summoned mental images of their hilarious hero, they also beckoned visions of Wanda Wiggins, the waddling blissfully inept secretary, and Eunice the world-class whiner in her ratty old flower-print dress. And as smiles spread across their faces, they could vividly picture Carol's Scarlett O'Hara character standing straight-faced in her homemade gown made of curtains...complete with a huge curtain rod stretching out across her shoulders.

"Say Goodnight, Gracie"

The wonderfully wacky world of Burns and Allen

As the newly formed comedy duo premiered their act in Newark, New Jersey's Hill Street Theater, they both felt comfortable with their roles. After all, they each had considerable experience in vaudeville and had thoroughly practiced this new routine. On that evening in 1922, they knew just what to do. The perky little five-foot Gracie Allen, would deliver the straight lines. In response, her gruff-voiced partner, George Burns, would puff his cigar, arch an eyebrow, and deliver the punch line.

Despite their extensive practice, something was going wrong. The audience's reaction was completely backwards. They were laughing at the straight lines instead of the punch lines. "The first night we had 40 people out front," Burns later recalled, "and they didn't laugh at one of my jokes. But every time Gracie asked me a question, they fell out of their seats." There was just something about Gracie that had the little audience in stitches the minute she opened her mouth. Apparently they were still too busy laughing at her delivery to even catch George's funny lines.

As George shook his head and contemplated the situation, he realized he had to change something in the act. He could either pout and tell his new partner to stop hogging the spotlight, or roll with the flow and turn Gracie into the one with the funny lines. He realized that she wasn't trying to dominate the act, but simply had a natural comedic style. Since Gracie beamed with a lovable simplicity, George felt she might be perfect for what at the time was often called a "Dumb Dora" routine.

Although Gracie was definitely not a *ditzy blond* like the act called for, he thought she might be ideal for the role. She was, in fact, as one admirer later put it, "*ditzy* like a fox." Fortunately for their millions of future fans, George chose not to pout, but to simply flip the act around, becoming the straight man and letting Gracie get the laughs.

George wrote the material and Gracie would bring it to life with her wide-eyed innocent delivery. Her sincere style made even the most illogical questions and statements seem as if they made perfect sense to her. "When I was born," she declared with a totally straight face, "I was so surprised, that I didn't talk for a year and a half." As the audience took in her "Gracieisms," George's unflustered acceptance of her bizarre reasoning added punch to the joke. When he asked her why she had suggested that he give her mother a bushel of nuts – since she hadn't given him anything, her twisted logic again surfaced. "Why George," she patiently explained, "she gave you *me*, and I'm as good as nuts."

During the decades to come, George and Gracie would rise to the top tiers of comedy in vaudeville, radio, movies, and television. Even their first meeting, at the Hill Street Theater, had been funny. A friend of Gracie's pointed out the vaudeville team of Burns and Lorraine, and told her they were breaking up. The reason for the split, she informed Gracie, was that "Burns is terrible."

Gracie's show business dreams were not exactly coming true at the time. She had been performing since the age of three in various acts, primarily with her three sisters in Irish dancing and singing performances. She had recently left the group after a dispute with their bookers, the Larry Reilly Stock Company. Gracie decided to turn her sights toward a more *legitimate* future and enrolled in secretarial school. Somehow, though, she just couldn't extinguish the flames of her performing aspirations, so she decided to look into the potential vaudeville gig with Lorraine.

Mistakenly walking up to George later, she told him she heard he was looking for a new partner. He said he was, and set up a breakfast meeting for the next day. He was a bit confused, though, when Gracie smiled and said, "Thank you, Mr. Lorraine." Sensing she wanted to work with his partner, rather than him; George didn't correct her for several days. Despite what she had heard about Burns from her friend, Gracie decided to stick with the act when he told her his real name three days later. Besides, they seemed to be a good fit. George would furnish the path for Gracie's return to the stage. And although, at twenty-seven, he was ten years her senior, he realized she was a natural for the variety act. "She could sing, she could dance, and she was willing to work cheap," he reflected, "Who cared how old she was?"

Once they hit the vaudeville circuit and switched their roles in the comedy part of the act, they were off and running. The money wasn't much, but they were both used to that. Like his new partner's Irish dance routines, George had tried out a number of variety bits. Early on, he appeared on the vaudeville stage as a "trick roller skater." He didn't exactly set the show-biz world on fire, and since his less-than-complimentary reviews followed him around the circuit, he kept changing his name. But whether he skated as Willie Delight, Captain Betts, or Buddy Links, he never inscribed his name in the annals of roller skate superstardom.

During the next few years, they kept afloat in the vaudeville scene, never as headliners, but at least on the bill with them. Then, when the flickering images of early movies suddenly started to talk, Warner Brothers studios started filming short features of vaudeville stars, called Vitaphone Varieties. Burns and Allen quickly earned a reputation as a "disappointment act." This was an act that could fill in at a minute's notice when the headlining act wasn't able to make it to a filming. During their first short feature, in 1929, they filled in for an unavailable Fred Allen, performing their patter-and-dance bit in a routine called *Lambchops*.

Their immediate availability paid off. Starting the next year, they joined Paramount Studio's roster, turning out a string of one-reel comedies. Just as with their vaudeville skits, George usually wrote the bits and Gracie simply played *Gracie*. As always, she had her lines down pat and never needed direction. "I would ask the director, 'Where do you want me?' " Burns recalled, "and he would guide me to a spot outside Gracie's light." Paramount loved their film shorts and in 1932, included them in a full-length feature titled *The Big Broadcast*, which featured the nation's hottest radio personalities.

That spot foreshadowed their future. After several appearances on variety shows hosted by entrenched regulars like Rudy Vallee and Guy Lombardo, NBC offered them their own show. As they faced the studio microphone on January 4, 1933, with slightly trembling scripts in hand, they ignited a fuse of show-biz dynamite, which would blast them into the rarified realm of national stardom. Then, suddenly, that blast began to dim as the 1940s rolled around. Their radio format had followed their vaudeville routine, featuring two single people joking around and sometimes flirting a bit. Their audience, however, knew they were actually happily married with two adopted children. The ratings began to erode.

George realized they needed to make major changes in the show. In 1941, the reorganized "New Burns and Allen Show" featured them as a married couple in more of a situation comedy format. The restructuring worked perfectly. Their radio ratings, as did their later television ratings, soared near the top and remained there until Gracie's 1958 retirement. As Gracie observed her world through her slightly blurry mental lens, and George walked out of the scene to talk directly to the viewers, those viewers were right where they wanted to be – in the wonderfully wacky world of Burns and Allen.

The Birth of the Bambino

Babe Ruth's journey from trouble maker to record breaker

It's not as if the boy in question had pulled off an armed robbery or shot someone. A lot of teenage juvenile delinquents did what young George had done – skipped school, swigged beer, chewed tobacco, and engaged in petty thievery. As the Baltimore city authorities made their decision to place him in St. Mary's Orphanage and Reformatory, they knew he wasn't an orphan. But George's mother was often sickly, and his father worked long hours in his seedy waterfront bar. There was another fact to be considered when the city officials placed him in St. Mary's as an "incorrigible." George was not a teenage delinquent – he was, in fact, only *seven years old.*

According to reports, George was admitted to St. Mary's for a variety of "bad behaviors." One of these, however, would play a huge role in his future. During games of street ball, he was always breaking windows of local buildings with his long-distance hits. As the attitude-drenched boy entered the reformatory, he encountered the stern faces of the Catholic monks who ran it. One of these, he learned, was Nova Scotia-born Brother Matthias Boutlier, the school's Prefect of Discipline.

Despite the daunting title, Brother Matthias was well liked and respected by the kids for his firm but fair attitude. The muscular six-footer was not a stereotypical mild-mannered monk. For one thing, he was very athletic and loved the game of baseball. He and the scruffy street boy bonded almost instantly. This was curious due to Matthias's role as the school's disciplinarian and young George's role, as biographer Robert Creamer put it, as "one of the great natural misbehavers of all time."

Ruth was encouraged to join St. Mary's baseball team on his first day there. The school's athletic director, Brother

Herman, put him in the game as a catcher and later played him at third base and shortstop. Despite being a leftie and needing to make do with a right-handed glove, young George began to shine at the game. Most afternoons, Brother Matthias would grab a well-worn baseball and swat fly balls to the boys. As he gripped the bat tightly near the end and took a powerful swing, his protégée snapped a lasting mental photograph. "I think I was born as a hitter," Ruth once reflected, "the first day I ever saw him hit a baseball."

As the hard-crusted street boy grew into a teenager, some of his rough edges were smoothed off by the St. Mary's staff. Again, Brother Matthias played a crucial role. His naturally calm and empathetic personality, like his athletic prowess, provided a positive role model for the young hell-raiser. "He taught me how to read and write," Ruth later said, "and he taught me the difference between right and wrong." "He was the father I needed," Ruth solemnly declared, "and the greatest man I've ever known."

Some today might question how successful Brother Matthias and his fellow monks were at teaching their young charge *right from wrong*. As the years stretched out, Babe Ruth, as history would come to know him, was equally known for his inimitable baseball skills and his all-night carousing and womanizing. His personal flaws, however, were counterbalanced by a lifetime string of unpublicized visits to children's hospitals and orphanages. Often, he would sponsor a bus full of orphans to join him at the stadium. In fact, even following one of his all-night binges, he could usually be seen trying to focus his reddened eyes on the priest during morning mass at the nearest Catholic Church.

It was Ruth's pitching that first caught the attention of the Baltimore media. Early on, Brother Matthias noticed him snickering at the bumbling attempts of one of the team's pitchers. "Go in and see if you can do better," Matthias challenged him. He not only did better, he was soon chosen as their starting pitcher. At 18, in 1913, he began playing against other teams in the community. Area sportswriters reported on his pitching abilities as well as a knack for slamming home runs.

The Baltimore Orioles, at the time, was a minor-league team in the International League. History is cloudy about exactly how Ruth came to the attention of their manager, Jack Dunn, but one thing is clear. After watching Ruth play for less than an hour in February of 1914, Dunn was so impressed he signed him to the roster. Dunn was known for working with younger players who showed potential. Ruth's teammates jokingly referred to him as "Dunn's newest babe." That would prompt the most famous nickname in baseball history – Babe Ruth.

As the 1914 International League's regular season began, Ruth pitched well and gained a reputation for being dangerous at the plate as well. As Dunn watched his star player, he knew that when young Babe Ruth fixed his piercing brown eyes on a ball and pursed his pronounced lips, that every ounce of his concentration was focused on slamming it over the right field fence. Unfortunately, Dunn also knew that an outing to see the Orioles play was not exactly the hottest ticket in town. Team attendance sometimes dipped to as few as 150 fans. Dunn had little choice but to sell his best players to obtain the funds to keep the team alive. He sold Babe and two other talented pitchers to the American League's Boston Red Sox.

Year by year Ruth garnered a legendary baseball reputation as well as a string of nicknames. Sportscasters and fans across the country began to christen their hero with epithets such as The Colossus of Clout, the Prince of Pounders, and the Wizard of Wham. For obvious reasons, most of them faded into history. One that didn't came from his Italian fans who loved their "Bambino." Ironically, within only five years, the Red Sox would sell him to the New York Yankees. During his time with the Sox, he helped them clinch three World Series championships.

Harry Frazee, the Sox' owner, also produced Broadway plays. As a result of several *Broadway bombs*, he seemed to always be strapped for money. Not coincidentally, the deal with the Yankees included a large personal loan for him. Following the trade, the Red Sox would face an 86-year championship drought which would forever be blamed on the team's management bringing about "the curse of the Bambino."

Conversely, the Yankees, who had never won a league championship, soared like one of Babe's out-of-the-park homers. Ruth's batting was red hot in the 1920 season, and the Polo Grounds, where they were playing at the time, surged with screaming overflow crowds. They were seldom disappointed, especially on May 1st of that year when Ruth rocketed a ball out of the stadium; a feat only attained previously by Shoeless Joe Jackson of the Chicago White Sox.

Before his seasons in the sun dimmed, Ruth led the Yankees to seven American League pennants and four World Series championships. During the mythical Yankee's season of 1927, the first six players in their batting lineup, which included Ruth and Lou Gehrig, were tagged as "Murderer's Row." In that same year, Babe Ruth set a season home run record of 60, which would stand for 34 years.

As he set and re-set 56 major league records, including 714 lifetime homers, legends and myths grew around him. Sadly, the famous 1932 "called shot" when he pointed to centerfield before slamming a home run there, seems to fall into the latter category. Regardless, he definitely *called the shot* of his inimitable career early on. When asked if he minded playing nearly every position during his St. Mary's days, he foreshadowed his lifetime passion. "It was all the same to me," he said, "All I wanted to do was play."

A Lucy-lovin' Nation

The origin of *I Love Lucy*

The lovable but brash redhead didn't seem to understand what she was asking for simply wasn't possible. She would need to decide – either use a live audience *or* a multi-camera shoot. Nobody had ever combined the two. After all, she and her husband, Desi Arnaz, had decided to shoot their television show like a play from the beginning to the end, complete with an audience. Everyone in the television business knew that using more than one camera required different lighting and lens distances for each shooting.

They would need to repeat each shot several times as television programs had always done during a multi-camera production. The audience couldn't be expected to maintain enthusiastic laughter with each successive take. It was time for veteran cinematographer, Karl Freund, to set both Lucy and Desi straight. Employing his firmest professional voice, he furrowed his brow, set his jaw, and emphatically repeated what he had previously told them. "It can't be done!"

Lucy and Desi, however, had a powerful weapon in their arsenal – their combined charm. Lucy fluttered her lashes over pleading blue eyes while Desi flashed his disarming smile. Then, sensing a slight crack in Freund's defense, Desi fired the big gun – flattery. "Well, I know that nobody has done it up to now," he crooned, "but I figured if there was anyone in the world who could do it, it would be Karl Freund." Knowing he was done for, Freund shook his head and set to work on the task that *couldn't be done.*

Desi's evaluation of Freund's abilities had been accurate. Issue by issue, he tackled and eventually solved each problem. Freund used various shades of gray paint to *paint out* inappropriate shadows that might appear with the variations in lighting. He and newly hired director, Marc Daniels, strategically positioned four cameras with differing lenses. They hoped the audiences wouldn't mind occasionally peering over and around the equipment to see the show. Unfortunately the necessary modifications to the studio, especially enlarging the building to comply with fire regulations for the expanded seating, would considerably increase the show's cost. CBS balked at the extra expense.

Always the wheelers-and-dealers, Desi and Lucy offered to take large pay cuts to make up the difference...with one *small* stipulation. They wanted 80% ownership of the filmed episodes. CBS readily agreed. After all, they figured, once the shows were aired, the film they had shot them on would be worthless. History, of course, has shown them to be just a tad short-sighted. That short-sightedness would eventually turn Lucy and Desi into television's first millionaire television stars. When nostalgia for the show brought about syndicated re-runs, the "worthless film" transformed into solid gold.

That kind of wealth was new to both of them. In fact, Desi had begun his working life cleaning bird cages for a man who sold canaries to pet shops. His family had fled Cuba in 1933 with little more than the clothes on their backs, when Batista overthrew the Cuban government. Like the rest of his family, he took whatever job was available. Although Lucy began a little higher on the job ladder than a bird-cage cleaner, the Jamestown, New York actress-to-be worked more than her share of extra and bit parts before Lady Luck finally appeared. Lucy acted in so many second-rate B movies during the 1930s, she gained the nickname, the "Queen of the Bs."

The pairing of this unlikely couple transpired in 1940 during the filming of the Rogers and Hart musical, *Too Many Girls*. Desi had been performing in the Broadway stage version when RKO pictures bought the film rights. To cast the part of Arnaz's love interest in the upcoming movie, RKO turned to their *Queen of the Bs*. As filming began, their on-screen love affair quickly spread to real life. Following a whirlwind four-month courtship, Lucy and Desi were no longer just costars; they were a real-life married couple.

While Desi toured the country with his Rumba band, Lucy continued her acting career, eventually settling into a successful stint on CBS radio with a popular radio show, "My Favorite Husband." In 1950 CBS decided to move the comedy to television, and asked Lucy to make the move. She was enthusiastic about the idea, but told them she would only go if her husband was hired as her co-star. The network executives said that pairing a beautiful New York redhead with a Cuban bandleader wouldn't seem a realistic couple – despite the fact that they were married in real life.

In order to prove that people would accept the concept, they worked a vaudeville-type act into his tour dates. Partway through the band's musical numbers, Lucy would appear – wandering around on stage, carrying a cello, and sporting a bewildered look. She was scheduled to audition, she told a flustered Desi Arnaz. Following this, the couple would break into their comedy skits, leaving the audience in stitches and the critics eventually convinced television audiences would accept their marital roles.

With CBS on board, they began searching for actors, writers, cameramen, and all the rest. But another concern soon arose. CBS liked the name *The Lucille Ball Show* for the title. Lucy, however, had decided Desi's name should not only be in the title, but should come before hers. The network, however, simply wouldn't buy *The Desi Arnaz and Lucille Ball Show* for the name. Once again, it seemed their program planning had hit a dead end. Finally, someone devised a creative way to work Desi into the title first. He would obviously be the "I" if the show was called *I Love Lucy*.

Once this had been solved, the talent search continued. Lucy actually wanted her fellow actor on *My Favorite Husband*, Gale Gordon, to play the role of the crabby neighbor and landlord, Fred Mertz. Gordon, though, was tied up with the *Our Miss Brooks* radio program. William Frawley, who had met Lucy previously, telephoned her when he learned about the upcoming show and asked if there might be a part for him. Similarly, Vivian Vance was not the network's first choice for Fred's wife, Ethel. Lucy had worked with Bea Benaderet in radio and wanted her to play the part. Like Gordon, she was busy with another role – playing Blanche Morton on television's *Burns and Allen Show*. Looking back, though, it's hard to conceive of better selections than Frawley and Vance for the roles of the Mertzes.

For six rollicking years, most of the nation peered through small magic windows to observe the black and white world where Lucy, Desi, Fred, and Ethel mined their comedic gold. That immortal goldmine still reflects classic scenes that seem to shine with an increasing luster as the years roll by. Among those immortal images is the one of Lucy and Ethel stuffing chocolates into their pockets...and eventually their mouths, as an out-of-control conveyor belt speeds the candy by them. The shimmering views also include images of their wild grape-stomping as well as their tango-dancing calamity after they had hidden raw eggs in their blouses. They also display Desi and Fred's kitchen disaster as they dodge falling chickens the overzealous pressure cooker had blasted to the ceiling, while a boiling pot prepares to spew a floor full of slippery rice.

The adulation of their millions of fans is corroborated by the show's consistently high ratings. During their run from October, 1951 to May of 1957, they often garnered as much as 60 to 70 percent of the viewing audience. In addition, along with *The Andy Griffith Show* and *Seinfeld*, it was one of only three shows to go out in the number-one position. But those millions of fans don't need any statistics to validate their loyalty. Their justification is easy – they simply *love Lucy*.

"Smile Because it Happened"

The whimsical career of Dr. Seuss

There actually wasn't much for Marco to tell about his walk home from school, down Mulberry Street – just seeing a broken-down wagon drawn by a horse. But the imaginative little boy couldn't simply relay that boring vision to his dad. No, before he told his tale, he would have to perk it up a bit. As a gleam lit up his eyes and a smile turned up the corner of his mouth, the "perking" began.

Suddenly, the horse transformed into a zebra and the wagon into a golden chariot. Then, the wagon became a fancy sleigh. Soon the zebra changed into a reindeer. Without notice, the sleigh turned into a sparkling bandwagon sporting a lively brass band. It would need to be pulled by an elephant, Marco decided. As his imagination clicked into high gear, he began to select the perfect pachyderm. "I'll pick one with plenty of power and size, a blue one with plenty of fun in his eyes," Marco decided. "And then just to give him a little more tone, have a Rajah, with rubies, perched high on a throne."

Before Marco's inventive mind finished with the mundane horse and wagon he had seen slogging down Mulberry Street, the scene shimmered with excitement. The elephant was soon joined by two giraffes and a squadron of policemen on motorcycles to escort the assemblage past the mayor and an alderman. As they pranced along, a shower of confetti rained down on them. Before he could tell his dad the inflated version of his walk home from school, though, Marco burst his own fantasy bubble. His father, he sadly decided, would never believe his made-up tale. When his dad inquired about what Marco had seen on his walk home, the dejected little boy just dropped his head and told the boring truth:

" 'Nothing,' I told him, growing red as a beat, 'but a plain horse and wagon on Mulberry Street.' "

Little Marco's dejection was eventually felt by the writer and illustrator who had created him. In fact, following the 27th rejection of the illustrated manuscript, "And to Think That I Saw it on Mulberry Street," Ted Geisel knew exactly what to do with it – *burn it!* As he strode down a sidewalk in his hometown of Springfield, Massachusetts, a "Grinch-like" frown occupied his forlorn face. The vivid images of Marco, the elephant, the giraffes, the Rajah, and all the rest were replaced with that of a flaming pile of crumpled typing paper. His mind was made up. Marco had to go up in smoke.

The mental image of the blazing manuscript, however, quickly morphed into a real-life view of an old friend approaching him as he walked down Springfield's Madison Avenue. Mike McClintock, his former college buddy, struck up a conversation. While they talked about their lives since their Dartmouth College days, Ted learned his friend not only worked as an editor for Vanguard Press, but was in their Children's Books department.

After exchanging pleasantries, Geisel told McClintock about the string of editor's rejections of his manuscript. In response, McClintock asked to see it. This time, the verdict was different; he liked it. The resulting book would plaster smiles across the faces of hundreds of thousands of children and their parents. In addition, it would ignite the career of a beloved writer who would color the world with the iconic images of a cat in a hat, a Christmas-hating Grinch, and a plateful of green eggs and ham – Dr. Seuss. Theodore Seuss Geisel later reflected on the chance meeting saying, "That's one of the reasons I believe in luck. If I'd been going down the other side of Madison Avenue, I would be in the dry-cleaning business today."

Lady Luck may have smiled on him that day in 1937, but she had pretty much ignored him for several years before that. His journey toward publication began as a child. Inheriting his love of words from his mother and an artistic streak from his father, young Theodor began to exercise both abilities. His father was Superintendent for the city's Parks Department and ran the Forest Park Zoo. Theodor and his sister, Marnie, often accompanied him to work. Already brimming with creativity, young Theodor drew the animals and enhanced them on his sketch pad with long necks, droopy ears, and silly smiles.

His mother, Henrietta, had sold pies in her father's bakery. As she hawked the pastries, she did so in a rhythmic meter. The same comforting tempo found its way into the stories and poems she read to Theodor and Marnie. Theodor soon began to replicate the sound with made-up nonsense rhymes.

His love of creating odd little cartoon characters grew as he matured. While attending Dartmouth College, he often doodled during his classes more than he took notes. His father soon voiced his dismay over his son's faltering grade average. In response, young Theodor buckled down with his studies and even became the editor-in-chief of the school's humor magazine, *Jack-o-lantern.* His fellow magazine staff members admired his knack for drawing wacky cartoons.

His position at the magazine soon disappeared when he and several friends were caught drinking gin in his room. The infraction was enhanced since this was during the Prohibition era. One of the punishments allotted was to be taken off the *Jack-o-lantern* staff. Always innovative, Theodor continued drawing cartoons for the magazine under a penname. He signed his cartoons with his middle name, which was also his mother's maiden name, "Seuss."

Since he had improved his grades, Geisel decided to become a college English professor. Following graduation from Dartmouth, he enrolled at Oxford and set his sights on obtaining a doctorate in English Literature. Soon, though, he decided his pathway to success would likely not include academia. His feelings were supported by a classmate, Helen Palmer, who steered him toward drawing as a career. He soon dropped out of college, proclaiming it "astonishingly irrelevant" to his goal, and focused his attention on writing and illustrating. His career would not be the only thing Helen influenced. In November of 1927, they married. Years later, with tongue-in-cheek, he decided to give himself a doctorate in name only, and would begin using the name, Dr. Seuss.

It would be a decade before Geisel launched his children's books. For several years he worked for the humor magazine, *Judge,* and also sold illustrations and cartoons to *Vanity Fair, Life, Liberty*, and other national magazines. Both Ted and Helen loved to travel and in 1936, during a European voyage, he began to write a children's poem to the rhythmic drone of the ship's engines. The result was "And to Think That I Saw it on Mulberry Street."

Several of his classic books similarly sprang from chance incidents. In the mid-fifties, Houghton Mifflin's Education Division director, gave Geisel a long list of words he felt children should learn at an early age. He then challenged Geisel to use them to "write me a story that first-graders can't put down." The result, "The Cat in the Hat," remains a classic page-turner. Five years later, publisher Bennett Cerf bet Geisel he couldn't write a children's book using fifty or fewer different words. Not only did Geisel win the bet, but launched the best-selling "Green Eggs and Ham."

Although Dr. Seuss is no longer around to produce his parade of one-of-a-kind characters, they continue to entertain children and their parents around the world. As we smile at the Cat in the Hat, Horton the elephant, Sam-I-Am, the Grinch, and all the rest, it is only natural to mourn the absence of their creator. Most likely, though, he would give us the same advice he once used for the title of one of his many popular books: "Don't cry because it's over, smile because it happened."

Index

Made in the USA
Middletown, DE
16 September 2023